Published by:

M

MERCURIA PRESS
www.mercuriapress.com

an imprint of

CHIN MUSIC PRESS
1501 Pike Place #329
Seattle, WA 98101-1542
www.chinmusicpress.com

Book design by Carla Girard
Cover illustration by Julie Benbassat
www.juliebenbassat.com

First (1) edition
Printed in the USA

ISBN: 978-1-63405-993-0
Library of Congress Control Number: 2022930081

Possums
Run Amok

a true tale told slant

by
Lora Lafayette

Mercuria Press
2022

Tell all the truth but tell it slant

Tell all the truth but tell it slant —
Success in Circuit lies
Too bright for our infirm Delight
The Truth's superb surprise
As Lightning to the Children eased
With explanation kind
The Truth must dazzle gradually
Or every man be blind —

Emily Dickinson

Tied to the Wall

I measure escape like
Frightened snapdragons posing
For winter frostbite.
I can judge acuity
By leaning over a fire

And listening,

Growing loudly in warmth
Or practicing failure,
Mad watch of the false start,
Skin ripping like ripe plums
And punishing my heart

And finishing.

                          Lora Lafayette

Possums
Run Amok

a true tale told slant

by
Lora Lafayette

1

POSSUMS RUN AMOK

So, we emerged from a sort of salt watery, barren-of-life suburbia. An unviable place that we could never seem to navigate and where we had never fit in. Until finally we could trek into the much more eclectically pleasing life of the city in the riotous early days of punk rock. Every day we would quit school, a prison in both feature and function, and climb into Blim's van (custom-painted like a 70s version of a Diego Rivera mural) and head for adventure, or the closest thing to it that we could find. I remember lime Jell-O and Nutty Buddies with a rock 'n' roll lead singer and striking bizarre poses on the stairwell, doing the Mexican Hat Dance in a long dusty corridor around a huge sombrero, and a drummer who ate hundred-dollar bills until the bartender served us. I remember enjoying a brief trip to Seattle, trying to fish for sharks from the pier at the Edgewater Hotel with a guitarist and thinking up lyrics to our own punk rock songs—"Emphysema Rat" and "My Ranch-Style Home in Hazel Dell." And we started a fanzine with news about the punk scene in Seattle and song lyrics and pictures of bands and Pop Rocks packets.

Kay, my sister Sue and Blim were the oldest: the girls—fifteen; Blim—seventeen. Dasha and I were slightly younger at thirteen. Never were any of us asked for ID when buying alcohol or cigarettes, so it's not very surprising that older men didn't feel too lecherous while gratifying themselves; and they paid handsomely. We had sex only for money or on occasions when it wasn't expected of us, preferring abstinence when it was. We set ourselves apart from the world of "Breeders!"

We made Blim wear makeup; he didn't mind. We painted his eyelids stark blue, attached spidery eyelashes, and brilliant red lips sealed the facade. He most certainly didn't mind when we practiced oral sex on him, so that we might better our professional performances to maximize the financial reward. It was easy income. Better than what we'd had from shoplifting and the meager sums dished out by impoverished parents.

I was puzzled, albeit relieved, that my parents never even seemed to notice my extensive expensive wardrobe or my collection of around four hundred records, the jewelry, the perfume... They never questioned me when I was out of my mind on LSD, even when I was caught by Kay's mother while pontificating at length over the meaning of a TV test pattern. Or when sobbing with laughter after smoking some acrid, stale-smelling pot that was sold in "lids"—two-fingered lids, three-fingered lids... The parental units did sometimes confront me when I was perfectly sober (though it must be said that my sobriety was often akin to mania).

Those were the days before most sexually transmitted diseases could be irreversible and fatal, and there was much promiscuity between us and our many homosexual, transvestite, and transsexual friends. One of whom, Christy, a beautiful woman, had become female so that she could be a lesbian, and it must be said that sex with her was most explosive.

Kay and Sue developed quite a skill for clothing and making up drag queens. Dasha wanted to be one. Kay herself looked so much like one that the manager of an all-night restaurant (where we mostly ate Tapioca Royales and spooned down coffee with lots of cream) refused to let her use the women's room. Another time, when Blim and I emerged from a lovely powder room in a upscale hotel, the manager, to whom we apparently looked odd and out of place, confronted us: "What were you two girls doing in the ladies' lounge?" To which the bedecked Blim interjected, "I'm not a girl!" And the manager stared after us, mouth agape, with nothing more to say as we exited the lobby.

We decked my seven-year-old twin brothers in extravagant drag dress and toted them to nearby grocery stores, where we stole cheap cigarettes.

Blim's brain proved to be unsettled by all the drugs he took, and he ended up spending his time either in jail or the state hospital, repeating himself constantly—sometimes practical things like "Where are the cigarettes?" and sometimes "Remember when we used to go to the bank for free?" unable to understand even the basics of conversation.

The inconvenience of home base in the suburbs, disturbing to us, and the inconvenience of hitchhiking becoming more bothersome, Dasha and I moved in with a good friend, Michael. We stayed in the corner of his downtown apartment, sharing an overstuffed chair, putting on music, smoking and drinking and entertaining each other variously. Michael always introduced us as "my pets."

Convinced that the city busses were aliens and upset at the conspiracy of parking meters that dispensed no gum, Dasha and I went on a crusade. We tried to finesse people into admitting guilt about wrongdoing and especially to uncover further trans-planetary aliens. We encountered a man acting suspiciously like an alien at a hotel's swimming pool one night; he was breaking every rule, including the one not to swim at night. He was wearing cutoffs, and he held a cocktail in one hand, a cigarette in the other. We were very suspicious, but he redeemed himself presently by knowing the words to several Alice Cooper songs.

Michael maintained that if one uttered the word "kinidegan" to an alien, they would attack you and probably kill you. Even most ambulances were involved; except for the ones named AA, which we knew meant Anti-Alien. (It supposedly stood for

American Ambulance.) He said there were aliens all around, so one should always refrain from saying that dangerous word. If, for instance, you blared it in a crowded arena, there would be at least a few aliens who would wreak havoc.

Our activities with rock stars did not go unnoticed by the band of mainstream groupies in town. One of them, Select Susan, railed on and on about us in a prominent local journal, culminating in "They're not real groupies; we call them possumettes." We thought it silly for her to be mad at us. She only offered sex as drudgery. And her response to us only served to catapult us to cult fame. Suddenly everyone wanted to be a possumette.

2

UNWITTING CIRCUS GROUPIES

Kay, Sue and I earned our keep at a metaphysical faire, at one of the smaller buildings surrounding a large arena. In exchange for running messages here and there and taking inexpensive tickets at the door, we had our auras photographed, our handwriting analyzed, and were instructed on how to spirit travel. This latter practice could be easy or impossible; your spirit just needed, especially when almost asleep, to get up. I later had a brief mastery of this task.

Almost in the backyard of the faire, in the parking lot of the huge arena, a circus was preparing to perform. We found ourselves instinctively sucked into this behind-the-scenes, afterthought life.

I've never been able to get used to clowns, as I believe is common. I find them frightening and most loathsome. Thankfully, not many milled about. I wanted to jump at them and scream, "You make me sick!"

The roadies let us climb on top of an elephant, pet the horses, and talk kitten speech to the tigers. I was at this time too carefree and ignorant to have my animal rights identity fully developed, so I was able to enjoy it.

We watched the bejeweled performers in their tights and diaphanous skirts; their life seemed quite fantastic. It seemed teeming with danger, but also frolicky and quite fantastic.

We contemplated joining up. We dreamed that we could learn to be acrobats, ride the decked-out horses, and tame tigers. A dream short-lived—we were told we were too young.

We showed them a good, although a.m., radio station. That night was long. We ended up at a not well attended but remarkable party held in a nearby, fairly rundown motel. The seedy afterlife exposed itself to us. Life teemed with danger, enticingly so. We smoked hash. This drug has never done well by me, and I should never have smoked it that night; it makes me too dizzy and actions play out like the flashes of a strobe light, a constant jolt to my nerves. My condition that night was worsened by a rather hearty consumption of alcohol.

Before stumbling to an escape walkway, I passed out. I had periods of awareness in which I realized I was known by more than one man, taking turns with my inert body, turning dead to the world. And who knows what happened after that. I regretted in the morning that I had been too stoned to charge them—I was cheated, an opportunity lost, a theft not thwarted. Ever since this interaction, circuses have had minimal appeal to me.

3

GROWING AWRY

Early on in life, I grew wild; I could not be controlled by any person or threat. We wandered the streets day and night and felt that the world belonged to us. We thrived on stolen doughnuts, expired produce and moldy Hostess pies, as well as illegally purchased alcohol or stolen bottles of cloying Thunderbird that was quick to intoxicate, and a constant supply of street drugs. I took any drug that was offered to me, often not even asking what it was.

We were considered, by the few professionals we talked to, disturbed. I think that out of all of us, Dasha came closest to filling that bill. She got kicked out of a therapist's office for reportedly lunging at her. She swung her "Billion Dollar Baby" (her tribute to Alice Cooper) doll menacingly at passersby. She yelled and struck out and generally frightened the young, the old, and all the in-betweens. She jumped on strangers, screaming, "Iota!"—demonstrating that you could bowl people over with a single iota. She grabbed a Look candy bar from Sue's hand, and when Sue protested, she got a chewed-up bolus spit in her face. Being Dasha, she chased me from the bedroom, down a hall, into the bathroom and cornered me in the bathtub, wielding over me a switchblade knife. We were best friends, but I had said something that offended her. I was covered with bruises for saying "Toyohiko Kagawa, 1888-1960, a Japanese social reformer and political leader." I'd repeated this aloud for a few moments in an attempt to memorize the dictionary, and for some reason this enraged her. Or once, I inspired wrath by saying "homologate" too many times. She worked in a small café, and whenever she could manage it, she stole the owners blind.

When she wasn't in a creative wrath, Dasha was in a creative mirth. Often enough, we encouraged each other to commit pranks, like shoplifting or spray-painting expensive automobiles with an anarchy emblem. Somehow I didn't realize these acts were illegal or would have any consequence.

In the middle of a night, on the spur of the moment, we decided to run away to hitchhike to LA. The trip was uneventful except for our growing hunger. At last we arrived, but with no baggage or money. Except for the few dollars dished out by the truck drivers who gave the longest rides, though there was always a condition of sex.

It was early evening when we arrived. We sat on a curb and wondered what to do next. For a while we just attacked offending palm plants.

Finally, a car of ambiguous make (some boat, seemingly pimp-owned) pulled up to our corner. We accepted the offered ride and headed off to the scene of our fanzine-indoctrinated dreams—Hollywood. The driver offered us a place to stay in exchange for favors; despite his lewdness, he let us out on Hollywood Boulevard with no complaint. We walked, scrutinizing the sidewalk, carefully noting the names in the long line of stars. All around, crime and commotion went on at tumultuous pitch. "Oh, look! Elton John!"

After a short while, a Mexican man approached us and invited us to his home. To entice, he promised drugs; we were tired and very hungry and gladly took him up on his offer. We walked to a VW van a few blocks away, and inside were three more young men; we packed ourselves neatly into the front seat. We rode for about fifteen minutes. We stopped and ordered Fillets o' Fish, washed down with cheap tequila.

We finally arrived at a worn red-brick apartment building. Everyone got out and climbed the four flights of stairs to a cockroach-infested hole. Joints were lit and there was tequila aplenty, and when we were nicely intoxicated, we were raped, as we had come to expect. At least we got grapes. The men didn't really hurt us—we were mostly just overpowered and threatened with a large knife. Date rape was soon becoming little more than an annoyance, one that we felt degraded the man more than us.

(I had once been told that I wasn't a good candidate for rape—curiouser and curiouser as this was proven untrue, repeatedly.)

Back on the street, in what was now full-blown night, we had no idea where to go or what to do. We wandered.

So we spent our hours, for the next couple weeks, walking around at night, sleeping in front of Hollywood High during the day, and eating stolen Zingers and Hostess pies. It was there that the pedophile manager of two semi-famous rock bands discovered us. His name was Ken Bowles. We moved in with him to a very attractive apartment with a pool in West Hollywood. Being weary of the streets, we didn't mind the sexual favors required, and Ken, in turn, took very good care of us. We were given new clothes; we were taken to concerts, sometimes rock, sometimes jazz; best of all—lots of drugs.

Our cozy situation ended when Ken was arrested for dealing heroin. We decided to return to Portland and stay with friends. So out came our thumbs, and we were on our way.

So, we made it to Grant's Pass, far into a sleepy, lead-headed night, when the car we were riding in backed into a police car in the parking lot of a diner where the driver had stopped for coffee. We ducked down in the backseat, trying to conceal ourselves. Of course, we were discovered and the driver gave us no cover, saying only that we were hitchhikers. The police grew suspicious and took us to the station.

When we arrived, the interrogation began:

"What's your name?" a burly officer asked me.

"Jane Woods," I replied. I had rehearsed for this moment.

"What's your middle name?"

Oops! I had forgotten to practice this with a middle name. My mind went blank.

"Jane... Jean, no, no... Jane May... Jane May Woods."

"What's your address?"

"2436 NW Burnside."

A few minutes later: "What's your address?"

"2832 NW Burnside."

"How old are you?"

"Sixteen."

"What's your birthdate?"

"September 25, 1952."

This would make me twenty-three.

"Are you sure?" they smirked.

"No, it was 1956," I corrected myself.

"Try again," but they left me alone.

Dasha wisely adopted the identity of an older friend. Her story, as a consequence, was straight. When the police called her father (who was a drunk), he said he didn't care where she was, that she was old enough to fend for herself.

On the strength of this, despite my poor performance, we were let go.

We were ecstatic—"the fools!" We laughed about my near fatal faux pas and headed back to the freeway to resume hitchhiking.

Before we got far, a state policeman pulled up and got out of his car:

"We've already been taken in and questioned by the local police."

"Well," he said, "I was just wondering why one of your pant legs is rolled up and the other isn't." Rolled-up bell-bottom pant legs were a sort of not-too-popular trend. My right one had fallen down. I gave the obvious explanation and he got back in his car and left us to continue our journey.

In Portland, we knew we could stay with our friend John. He did drugs in a mighty way—and he shared. His doctor only asked, "What would help?" then wrote the prescription, whatever it was. Back in the day, it was most often Quaaludes.

John did janitorial work at the seediest of porn palaces in the city. He worked in the wee hours of the morning. There was often money dropped on the floors by hard-up men fumbling to give lap dancers tips. Also a telling floor finding, small pools of semen drippings. Kay, Dasha, and I often accompanied John on his duties. We scanned the floor for money. John would turn on the theater's projectors, and we watched the hard-core films until we laughed too hard in disgusted hilarity or got too bored, "Breeders!" Then we would all go home, leaving the theater for the coming night's takers.

Feeling the need for education, I returned home to the ranch-style house. Even with parents and their attempts at rules, I was so awry that nothing could contain me, and my parents no longer tried. I told them when I was leaving and maybe which day I'd be back, and that was good enough. My bedroom was wallpapered in concert bills and magazine posters. I owned a stereo and a myriad of mostly stolen records.

I decorated myself in Alice Cooper makeup, glittery scarves and colorful skirts. My fellow student, Karin, once grabbed me from behind and tried to wash my face paint off; I got away. I was mostly left alone, for it was commonly thought that I was insane.

4

TIKHOKEANSKII

"Have you ever owned a car?"

"No."

"We did. Its name was Beads."

"Have you ever owned a dog?"

"No."

"We did. Its name was Beads."

"Have you ever owned an axe?"

"No."

"We did. Its name was Beads."

We were enamored of axes, especially the German word for it — "Axt!" — and our own axe, "Beads," which was apparently a popular Russian name for dogs.

"Hiya, Borges!" I yelled, upon entering a university's basement establishment known as Mother's Deli. Bottomless cups of coffee with honey were fifty cents and a huge pancake was served for seventy-five cents. And a constant flow of up-and-coming intellectuals crowded the bus-your-own tables. Kay and I jostled each other into the booth where Sue sat, now mortified. She was trying to affect a certain quality in hopes of impressing the potential suitor sitting with her. "My name is Susan," she had just told him—obviously her friends called her Borges. She hated that name, given to her because she loved the work of Jorge Luis Borges, but she resigned herself to the fact that our Cheech-and-Chong boisterousness would override any airs she might try to assume. She was studying French.

One of her good cohorts in pretension had asked me in a restaurant once, "Voulez vous du vin rouge? Ou du vin blanc?" And once, the frequently offensive Sue had declared at a party: "White Zinfandel is for trailer trash."

I hoped wholeheartedly that she was joking, but all night long her speech was peppered with French, and she never laughed. It was not the French I loathed, but American Francophiles.

Russophiles, on the other hand, were enjoyed and most welcome. My many letters to Brezhnev were sent with instructions on how best to invade the US. My favorite idea was that the Soviets could dig a tunnel under the ocean with a Roto-Rooter and invade insidiously with a plainclothes army. A Roto-Rooter employee, when asked, said with slow derision: "We don't deal in 'Roto-Rooters,' our *name* is Roto Rooter." My correspondence with Brezhnev was entirely one-sided.

On a trip across the river to Portland to purchase used clothes for fifteen cents a pound at a store called

As Is, we noticed a ship docked at the waterfront, which was then our turf. It was white—we figured it was only Coast Guard. But we scrutinized it, straining our necks, trying to make out the flag flying on the stern. I gasped and barely managed to suppress a scream, "Oh, my God! A hammer and sickle! It's Russian!" A Soviet ship, docked for our enjoyment. We could actually speak to Russians! We could toast the night with them!

It was through ballet, especially Nureyev, Nijinsky, and Pavlova, that I had developed a deep and enduring appreciation of Russia—Land of the Firebird—furthered by my adoration of Russian authors: Bulgakov, Tolstoy... Pushkin being one of the few I had never read; I don't know why. And my favorite short story of all was Gogol's "The Nose."

Kay and I rushed home to dress, the point being to shock. We slathered on as much depravity as we could—torn and written-on clothes held together with the punk icon—safety pins—disintegrating clear plastic shoes displaying differing loud and glittery socks, spiked black hair and, of course, there was no neglecting face makeup: black eye shadow and bright red lips, skin deathly white.

Not knowing what we were getting into, but greatly hopeful, we boarded the ship. What we hadn't expected and weren't prepared to meet was the Russian spirit head-on: generosity, kindness, vitality, life-lust; we were overwhelmed. Though I'd had a great appreciation of Russia before that, now I was a true Russophile. At the time, it meant that I was a "Red." And for a long time I was. (Until I realized that communism, and the same with anarchy, was unworkable.)

We spent the next five days on board that ship — the Tikhokeanskii (which meant "Pacific Ocean"). I had been celibate for some time, but I couldn't resist Sergei. "He's Russian!" I kept thinking — Russian! — and for once I enjoyed abstaining from celibacy. He lifted me easily into his upper bunk, my clothes seemed to fall off and we kissed deeply and stroked each other, becoming more and more entwined. He was beautiful and generous — we were laden with gifts.

We wanted to stow away or defect, though we didn't want to anger our parents (who still believed you could trust television news and that newspapers told only the complete truth). We toyed with the idea of harboring one of them as a pet in this country, but none of them agreed.

All the English from most of them was "Please! Please!" Misha was able to translate some more, and, with gestures and a dictionary, we managed to achieve great camaraderie. Sergei, playing a guitar, serenaded us with folk songs; one being about a horse on a ship, the ship hits a mine and explodes, the horse then drowns. We smoked the peculiarly Russian papirosas — a cardboard tube ending with a short, fat cigarette, very strong and hard to keep lit.

Dasha, after tasting their toothpaste, was compelled to hide under the sink. Then for no reason at all, she stood up on the seat of her chair. Her behavior prompted Misha to inquire, "Are you a hippie?"

We were treated to dine with them on hard candy that tasted like glue, some kind of meat that looked like feces and tasted likewise, bread smeared with literally inches of unsalted butter, tea with way too many melted rectangular sugar loaves, and wine with pieces of cork (we hadn't a corkscrew). The next day we shared with them some of our food, which happened to be slimy, moldy Hostess pies bought from a secondhand, at best, food store we depended on. My favorite — the bags of rotting Mounds bars. You could feast for under a dollar.

The appealing Pavel asked Kay from a phrasebook which social groups she belonged to. "Social?" she repeated, unsure of the question. "Oh," he said, satisfied somehow with that as an answer.

Kolya occupied himself by taking photos of our bare backs, while Kay wiped off the lipstick from where I had kissed the photos of Lenin and Brezhnev that lined the busy inner halls.

Potatoes were kept around the kitchen door to ward off hunger. Drafts were avoided at all costs, particularly the cold ones, which could kill. As could eating or drinking something cold on a hot day — the shock to one's system being too great. And flies spontaneously generated in unattended garbage cans.

At night we jumped off a boat dock, floating

a few yards in front of the "Tikh" in the polluted Willamette River. Or rather, the sailors pushed us off for sport, then jumped in, fortunately pulling us back out again, the river actually not fit for swimming and not equipped for easy swimming access. Then we froze until they gave us dry sweaters; the armpits of Kay's would become legendary in the world of odor and a favorite of our grey tabby cat, Rudy.

For those five days, we were deeply in bliss. Though the captain seemed to hate us, he tolerated us as we watched the propaganda films shown in the dining room — Soviet films about horses and gypsies. Yet he often sent guards to be sure we weren't on board after hours; though we were very loud, our sailors managed to hide us on these occasions. He would glare at us when we walked on the deck — one time he shook his fist and cursed us. Yet he endured. In our practically incoherent Russian, we called him what we thought was "fly," but as it turns out we were calling him "curtain."

I wasn't prepared for the hole it would leave in my life when they departed. The waterfront was cold and lonely. I wanted to go to the Soviet Union with every bit of will that I had. I cursed Brezhnev for not invading. I wanted to forsake my own culture and gain one infinitely more appealing to me. All we had now were some copies of *Soviet Life*, a paperback book of the Soviet constitution, the sweaters, a record of pop songs by Alla Pugacheva, some Belomorkanal brand papirosas, pins in the likeness of Lenin and the Soviet flag, and four cans of milk condensed with sugar.

We sought out similar good times on board Soviet freight ships that frequently docked in town, but though they were friendly and always gave us a tour, nothing ever came close to the Tikhokeanskii.

5

THE HOWLING FROG

Having missed most of the classes of my eighth-grade year, I would either be held back or, the only other possibility, I must attend an alternative school. Pan Terra was the most curative experience of my crumbled adolescence. The teachers liked my poem about vigilantes and being alone and Kay's picture (complete with story) of a potato car.

One of our "classes" was to volunteer somewhere. I chose the state school for the blind. There I worked with severely developmentally disabled and blind children around the age of ten. After weeks of pre-Velcro patience, I at last taught a girl how to tie her shoes. I was always proud of that.

It was the patient teachers at Pan Terra that finally helped me achieve my comprehension of algebra. They gave me back a gift I had discarded—an overwhelming desire to learn everything (except auto mechanics). They made me see a future, both serious and silly, but one in which meaning could prevail.

The other kids disliked us because we generally preferred creativity to drugs. It didn't help that Kay wanted to be a mortician—her mother wouldn't let her keep her textbooks on death in the house. And I wanted to be a CIA/KGB double agent. They, just like the mainstream kids before them, were extremely critical of our hairstyles and choice of clothing.

I realized that I needed more than Pan Terra could intellectually give me. I needed to return to mainstream high school to achieve something in my pursuit, my quest for knowledge. Mainly, I desired to take literature and writing classes and Russian.

I excelled in the writing class, though I really don't know what we were taught, just that my writing improved most markedly over the year. The instructor, a very interesting man, moonlighted at a drive-through spaghetti restaurant, a noble yet doomed attempt.

I turned out also to have a talent for acting; I was a finalist in a tri-state competition. My acting coach encouraged me to seek a career on stage. I was never scared on stage because those were not my words and my character could be the complete opposite of myself. But after all, my ambition lay elsewhere—I must write novels and poetry, and I must learn Russian.

The school I was attending had just that year dropped their Russian program, and no other high school in the area taught it. I was very upset. However, this proved to be serendipitous.

I learned that I could take the class at the local community college, high school grades weren't necessary for part-time study, so I enrolled. I spent hours listening to Russian folk and popular music. My favorites: "Arlekino" and "The Enamored Bandura Player." I begrudged any studying that took me away from my study of Russian. I saw every Russian film that I could. Studied the history. The glorious revolution—the people taking power, equality, camaraderie as a nation together and with other nations:

> *The last fight let us face,*
> *The Internationale*
> *unites the human race.*

I wanted to go—I would dream of standing in front of St. Basil's Cathedral, next to the Kremlin, surrounded by Russians and by Russia.

I discovered a few other classes at the college that I knew I would enjoy: Film Appreciation and Music Appreciation, wonderful classes both. Soon, I realized that I was going full-time to college. I wondered, what point was high school? I discovered that with a few college credits, high school achievement meant nothing—no need for GEDs or SATs or anything more than your college transcript. Kay and Sue had been living in the city for some time. I joined them. We enrolled part-time at Portland State University. We took Russian classes and German classes (for fun), Northern European Mythology, Russian Cultural History. I was completely intimidated—a University! I was surprised by my success. We took classes mostly for the fun of it—whatever struck our fancy, no thought to degree requirements or any other motive but interest, and we, on occasion, ignored the finals. I was only sixteen; I had no idea about course numbers, no thought of the difference between a 300 level course or 500. I thought all classes were equally matched. Therefore, somehow I found myself in a class called History of Political Theory. It was absolutely fascinating, and I did well in it. I later pointed it out to a friend who said, "That's a graduate class!" Quite the boost to my self-esteem. It was a university and I was doing well.

The Howling Frog was a very peculiar café. The baristas cared not how long one sat there, and they seemed annoyed when we ordered something. There was a huge bookshelf with many interesting volumes to be borrowed and returned, or not. They had various art shows there, usually grotesque or disturbing art. They played cult and underground music. It was a good place to read, even better to write.

Every Monday night they showed films in their back room. There was a lot of necrophilia, the corpses were brown and slimy—a long time dead. A beautiful young woman sucked a cloudy, discolored eye from a cadaver's socket. Dead mouths were made to pleasure dead penises. It was there that I saw *Faces of Death*, an extremely difficult film to find. And to watch. The only difference between it and a snuff film was that these deaths weren't staged, they just happened to be caught on film. I witnessed a woman being raped and murdered, a lit cigar pushed into a man's eye, a man executed in an electric chair (his eyes exploded). And especially hard for me, many horrors of the meat and fur industry. And the message of the film, repeated ad infinitum by the narrator: This is your destiny. This will happen to all of us. There is no escaping the horror—only denial. These images would haunt me, yet I sought them out, searching through libraries and cult magazines for more. Some later speculated that this film planted the evil seed that was slowly to grow and become the beginning of my spiral downward.

6

DANCING DEBUTANT

Kay and I liked to play fighter pilot atop an inner-city fountain and to sing operatic versions of Beethoven's *Ninth* and Borodin's *Polovtsian Dances* while skipping around on the architected slabs of concrete, often behind waterfalls.

We often gathered with Dasha, who enjoyed proving the logic of the absurd and to my surprise, knew the game of jai alai.

My first apartment was a studio. It was clean and warm and lit year-round with Christmas décor. I had Indian blankets over the sofa and draped over thresholds. I lit candles, even to read by, always preferable to electricity. I loved plants, but they always died from lack of sunlight, or too much water, or being thrown out high windows (thanks, Kay).

Lights from my own hallucinations would dance on the night-blackened, picture-covered walls. Often I would smell the strange, sweet smell that heralded a seizure, for which I took medication. The lights, however, kept darting and dancing and were sometimes disconcerting. The nedomtykomkas (little Russian devils) arranging themselves in corners.

Songs from The Partridge Family usually spilled from the speakers of my stereo; these songs overrode the deep depressions that continually threatened my stability.

Home was in the Northwest neighborhood. For a long while, it was made up almost entirely of students and old folk, the disabled and deformed and general misfits from society. There was The Ear, a man with half of his head rotting off; he was made to sit with the bad side of his head to the wall in the area's foremost diner. There was Mr. Stubbs, a man with most of both legs amputated; he had a very mean face, swore menacingly, and on his remaining stumps, often walked a big black dog. There was Wo, the neighborhood hooker, with her frosty pink lipstick, pastel blue eyeshadow, black and silver platform boots and bell-bottom Levi's; she picked up tricks on Burnside Street and hung out at Arby's. And there was Bob, the newspaper delivery man who'd had a lobotomy. He would always and only say, "Hi, how are you!"

Many times on routine trips to the grocery store, we would come across people felled and being kicked at by ambulance attendants. They were not always still alive. One man set a mountain of mangoes avalanching to the floor before him; I think he did die.

I developed a taste for baguettes with unsalted butter and Fromager d'Affinois; that and guava nectar were my healthy meal choice; more often Kay and I stuck with two pounds of M&M's (one with nuts and one plain) and two cans of diet soda (which made the checkout clerk smile). Or we tormented ourselves with our version of healthy: Sportsman's Mix, our favorite of the plentiful trail mixes. "Oh no, not the Sportsman's Mix!"

We spent an afternoon trying to gain the courage to push safety pins through our hands. We, at last, succeeded; we were initiated into the newest genre heralded by safety pins—punk rock.

One day, Kay and I were out carousing (probably on drugs—who knew?). Kay speedily darted a half block down the street under a darkened street lamp, just as Mr. Stubbs was passing by. When he got close she hurdled over him and we both ran off. Sue was mortified when we recounted the story, thinking we had "hurled" him.

We used to laugh a lot.

7

PUNK ROCK, IT'S TOO SLOW

Everyone, it seemed, either was in or wanted to be in a punk rock band—one of the beauties being you really didn't need to have skill or talent with voice or instruments, and the lyrics were pleasingly antisocial. Being attractive never mattered; people were praised for making themselves as ugly as possible. My favorite lyrics were those of The Mentors:

> *I want to do the secretary hump.*
> *I want to cram my dick up her rump.*

or

> *I'm a corn-shucker*
> *A real butt fucker*

and

> *Butt odor number nine.*

We had a club. The Revenge Club. Portland's venue for punk rock shows. Popular bands from around the nation played there. Though on opening night, there was a bit of a problem: the security guard (hired from a local biker gang) began hitting people, first the audience, next the performers.

Kay was hired to whip the members of a band

onstage, do a little song and then some sadomasochism. On her debut night, the police were called to quiet things down. They stood and stared at the onstage spectacle, a bit shocked it seemed. They told us to be quiet, then left, not bothered by the ticket taker's still-smoking bong.

Kay's biggest claim to fame was being Formica, lead singer of Formica and the Bitches, an all-girl band that included Sue on guitar. Their success was short-lived; none of them knew how to play.

We moved to a beautiful rented house in a residential neighborhood. There was a lush garden of a park, where the neighborhood kids played. The children were told to run inside if we came near; it's safe to say there was a bit of hysteria. We weren't quiet neighbors, and it became frequent for the police to be called.

One night when they came, I was nearly passed out on the porch, horrifiedly nauseated at the thought of moving at all, any part of my body. They just shined their flashlights at me and asked, "Is it dead or alive?" Thank God they left me, preferring to attack those who had tried to escape the premises out the back door.

Somehow everything got broken in the revels of every day and night. Fine, collected pieces of china were smashed on the street; the beautiful, leaded-glass windows were likewise smashed. Even a bathroom sink was wrenched from the wall. I left just in time to miss the lawsuit.

8

DREAMS OF FOREIGN SHORES

Kay, Sue and I met an interesting man named Larry. He had some money and wanted to open Portland's first underage gay discothèque. He proposed that if we helped him open and then run it, he would give us stock in the disco and a salary much higher than we ever hoped for.

Even though we hated disco, we worked long and hard painting and furnishing and generally decorating. Then the disco opened. I worked at the nonalcoholic bar, which was mostly serving coffee and soda to kids or anyone stoned out of their minds.

Sue worked as a disc jockey, though Larry hated the songs she picked out. "The Time Warp" was the patrons' song of choice. Multitudes would fill up the dance floor to reenact the famous scene of the then-quite-cult film favorite. Also people favored the newly emerging Village People.

Kay took care of collecting the door charge. Since this was a gay disco, and most assumed it was exclusively gay, it was rare to see heterosexuals, especially males. Kay was suspicious when two unfamiliar Arab men approached. They said, "We are feg." Kay had let straight men and women go by her that evening, but the enticement of fun made her request that they prove their sexual orientation by kissing each other. They refused and walked away angry. Also, it must be said that one had to be hypervigilant due to frequent gay bashings. One friend suffered especially, as he hit all the commonly bashed "isms"—a gay, black communist (though at least not a woman).

The three of us conserved our money, stringently saving every penny for a trip to foreign climes. We wondered why someone didn't come running blindly in, throw down tickets to Amsterdam, then run blindly back out again. But this was unnecessary; we managed to buy tickets to England after cashing in our stocks in the disco.

For some reason, Sue decided to go to New Orleans instead.

Kay and I left with enough money to carry us through for about a month. We didn't have tickets for the return home, but at the time we didn't care about returning; we just put our faith in fate.

9

FUN WITH COUNTRY

Somehow, when I looked out at the passing English countryside, I could easily see knights and kings in their various campaigns. I could see Dickens' dark world and Shakespeare's prolific and unsurpassed composing and could imagine Richard III trapped in the Tower.

London struck me strongly, more so than other foreign cities would, perhaps because it was my first. We rented a room in a lovely old mansion. It was close quarters, especially when the insane brother of the owner came home for his weekly visits. He was most adamant about having sex with Kay. He pursued her all over the house, until his sister put him back on the bus for Bedlam. Her husband continually burst into our room in the dead of night:

"You didn't win World War II! It was us that won World War II! I'm tired of the way you Yanks think you were the victors!"

"Go away! We don't care who won World War II."

He'd eventually pass out and the wife would get him back to their bedroom.

Kay and I both got jobs in a laundry factory, a very

stereotypical factory, such as Oliver Twist might have encountered. The windows were high and barred, and clouds of steam rose up everywhere. It was hot and the air, thick and stale. We washed royalty's poop-stained underwear. One day, while taking inventory of an order, Kay had not been able to find an item, perhaps as the word was foreign, but she got help: "Here's the red flannel, love!" The sentence stuck, and later our cat, another little gray tabby, was yclept Herestheredflannellove.

One day, tired of dragging it around, Kay and I stuck postage stamps and an address label on an otherwise naked handheld representation of the male sexual organ (named "Peppy") and put it in the post, bound for Sue — but it never arrived.

Kay had a sort of boyfriend named Richard; he called her Frolics and loved to hold her down and spit on her face then lick it off again. Our other boyfriends in London were always of the ground-kicking, unsure-of-themselves, endearing sort.

Our best friend was a Frenchman named Michel. He told us the meaning of the words to our favorite song *Ca Plane Pour Moi*. He was fortunate enough to be "on the dole"; he hadn't worked in years. He introduced us to rather prominent punk rockers; we even did some backup singing.

Kay's temper knew no bounds. Because I changed my mind about getting a loaf of bread, she plotted for the next few weeks to kill me — sleeping with a knife under her pillow. One day, after I turned down a previously-agreed-on pizza, she sent the table flying (because she wouldn't get the few cents off of her salad bar).

We developed a love of classical music and always rock, and then folk. We drove the tenants of our house mad with singing along to Pete Seeger's "Bought Me a Cat" and The Monkees' "Daydream Believer."

Enthralled with the idea that we could go anywhere, we dragged our bags to Victoria Station, then took the train to Dover.

Dover being a port town, we found ourselves in the bustle of the docks. Greeting sailors, but not just. We collected tidy sums on these trips to the merchant marines. Whenever we needed money, we had a way to supplement our incomes. And we always had fun; even our anger was only play, hilarious to us (though onlookers didn't get the joke of it); we were never bored.

"La casa... La sopa... El gato... Yo busco el parque Chapultepec, dónde está?"

Santos was hammering away at me and didn't seem distracted that my attention lay solely in mimicking his native tongue.

Afterwards, I roamed around the ship that Kay and I called "The Janeba."

"Excuse me, sir, but did you know that you've got a cucumber on your head?"

I was attempting to save Kay from rape; she had faux-pas-ed her way into a sticky situation. She had promised a man she would sleep with him if he gave her two hundred pounds. To her shock, he did! Yet she had no intention of sleeping with him and had suddenly, though momentarily, grown picky. He was irate. He pushed me away; Kay pushed him. She put her shoes on (the wrong way) and we ran up the laddery stairs, trying to find the way out. A few of the sailors tried to thwart our attempt to leave, but Santos, who had compensated Kay and me handsomely, turned out to be decent and showed us to the gangplank. And as we were leaving, Helg gave Kay a shirt she had coveted, a tee shirt with the stencil of an armadillo and the words "Evoludo No Gogo"—we were never positive what the Portuguese caption meant, but armadillos were Kay's favorite creatures. The sailors all stood on the deck yelling after us that they loved us:

"You're beautiful!"

"You're scum!"

"We'll miss you!"

"Fuck off!"

We made it home safely.

We began to notice the ability we had to drive anyone from a room in uncomprehending amazement. Why was Kay sitting there screaming, "My buttocks! My buttocks!" and pointing to them wildly? (Actually reenacted from an interview by Dick Cavett with Rudolf Nureyev.) We were freaks among freaks.

Nothing struck us as funny as something truly ugly (especially if it wasn't intended to be). So we played ugly music, sought out hideous works of art. Tormented ourselves, having sex with the repulsive.

We didn't stay in Dover long. Our funds were running dangerously low. We managed to glean enough from sailors, yet we were growing tired of meager living. The only work available without a proper visa was either the factory sort or full-scale prostitution—neither of which enticed us. We were homeward bound.

On returning to the States, I threw up all over the customs agent (I had eaten some semi-raw Colonel's chicken). I didn't feel bad about it; she was being horrible to us:

"Why are there no tags in your clothes? What kind of hair dye do you use? How much money do you have? Do you use tampons? Or pads?" And many other questions she had no right to ask, especially in such a bitchy tone.

My grandfather was a customs agent and he used to laugh a lot about the way he mistreated and humiliated people (especially women).

10

IT WAS A YEAR OF ECLIPSES
AND VOLCANOES

For the eclipse, we drove to the best vantage point, about seventy-five miles away to the east of Portland. The land was made up of treeless bluffs and grassy plains and stark outcroppings of rock. If you looked carefully enough you could see delicate little flowers in various colors. A lovely museum was nearby, with exquisite peafowl ready to sound the alarm on the rattlesnakes that abounded. There was supposedly a famed replica of Stonehenge nearby, but I never saw it.

The sun was veiled in shadow. Animals and birds, in reaction to the change, began to behave erratically. The cows stampeded back and forth. The birds flitted and flapped and couldn't settle down; nothing was still. The eclipse, though monotone, cast almost kaleidoscopic shimmerings on the ground. I was glad to have witnessed it. But it was very soon over.

The Wishram Cafe, at a popular train stop, served us coffee and eggs for cheap.

Afterwards, Kay and I set to climbing to the hilltops. It hadn't looked so daunting from the road, yet the further we climbed, the more the bluff seemed to rise. I kept hearing what I thought must be bees as I climbed over rocks, though I never could see one. Our discovery of the source of the buzzing was horrifying; we rested on a rocky outcrop, and I nearly put my hand on a rattlesnake—then, there was not just one, but a tangled, slithering mess. We fled. Mostly we slid down the bluff, as it was faster than trying to run.

We played on logs in Horse Thief Lake, trying to unbalance and knock each other off, then went home.

The volcano was impressive. We had been warned of a major eruption, but a few months after the eclipse, when it finally exploded, what had been the perfect cone of Mt. St. Helens was now completely beheaded, from graceful mountain to rocky stump. The inferno of ash boiling into the clear sky greatly dwarfed the remains, and lightning flashed everywhere in and around the crater. Forests were flattened in seconds, leaving landscape that in barrenness resembled the moon. Sightseers were warned for months to stay away, which had the opposite effect, and job-driven reporters were killed quickly—suffocating in ash several feet deep or burned by the swift current of searing hot mud—the result of melted ice and dense ash mixed with tree trunks and boulders; there was evidence that a few people had been vaporized.

Ash began to fall in the city. It was eerie, more silent than snow, though to the sight it seemed very similar.

There were scares about the toxicity of the ash;

people dared not go out without a mask or scarf covering their mouths and noses. Airplane and automobile engines were clogged with it; bridges were washed out by mud and debris, travel was difficult. The drear of the world's weather was blamed on our mountain—"Amerika's Vulcan ist schuld." My father reminded me that I'd had my chance to jump in—but I wasn't a virgin anyway, so it probably wouldn't have helped.

These various events rung in the year that would always remain my favorite. I was still a teenager, and the best time of my life was shortly to pass. At least I noticed its passing. And at least, if brief, it was remarkable.

11

THE BLEEDING HEART

"Save yourself, Rob!" we shouted out to the waiter. I had discovered a bomb… well, actually I thought it was a bomb, I'd only heard it, but Sue and the dishwasher Peter concurred. A beeping, regular and continual, interrupted my cooking. Rob sneered at us to be quiet and go back to work, though so vocal were our hysterical protests that several tables got up to pay their checks. A gentleman customer realized that it was his pager that had caused our distress. He apologized. But many people left their seafood Eggs Benedict anyway, perhaps never to return.

Rob caused the waitress Eve to cry by saying that she wasn't an anarchist. It was a silly thing to say, meaningless to a secure person, but Eve, perhaps, wasn't sure of her activist status. She crusaded a lot at work against Nazi style, fluoridated water and all commercialism. She was annoyed by my love of Western Family products, and she loathed my prolific ability to sing or quote advertisements.

Frequently, as I put plates of steaming food into the pass-through window, my boss Tom would call from the kitchen door, "Hey, Cookie!" Hurried, I would cast a glance at him; he would be doing a dance with his tool exposed, flapping it about in its flaccid state. I would always calmly grab my Mighty Oak (my favorite knife) and come after him with deliberate speed. At which time, he would repack himself and beat a hasty retreat.

He was quite good at answering questions. At a gathering of girlfriends, we all agreed that we had always wondered what it felt like for a man to pee. "I'll call Tom!" I decided. He was busy. He answered the phone in a clipped voice; it was the exact middle of his busiest shift. I put the question to him. He stopped, thought a moment, then said that a man can feel the stream flowing through his penis, yet the major sensation of having to relieve oneself comes from the bladder (like women). Some men find it difficult to "perform" in public urinals and freeze up. But it can be relieving to the point of mild euphoria, and it's possible for men to experience pleasure by peeing after sex. On the other end is the fire of communicable disease or kidney stone. We were also curious to ask more about the male experience of sexual intercourse, but we saved that for another day.

The morning after an attempt to exterminate the hordes of cockroaches, Rob told Sue and me that the cunning, greasy objects most hated always climbed to the ceiling to escape the spray, but eventually the fumes would catch up with them and they would fall like acorns. We spent that day cooking with one hand, the other keeping an umbrella shield overhead.

Clock worked as a host, despite his advanced degree in business. He was taking a respite from a "real job." Named Clock because he was the only one with the impossible task of always knowing the correct time (the restaurant clock was perpetually unreliable and eventually quit altogether). His wisdom in matters of life caused him to be bestowed with the further appellation of Wise Timepiece. He was good for serving "host's coffee" to the kitchen staff—Schwarze Katz wine served discreetly in coffee mugs. He enjoyed giving trout heads as presents to the unsuspecting and, for some reason, beating me on the head with a large white cheddar cheese.

Every time someone would put an "Out to Lunch" or "IQ of a Potato" sign on Rob's back, he would rage back to the kitchen and yell at me. Likewise, when a rotting tomato fell on his head as he opened a refrigerator, he broke an egg on my head in retaliation. Though it was an incident for which I was innocent.

We often came back to the darkened restaurant from frolics in gay bars. We poured ourselves the white German wine and made soufflés and quiche and sat in a large back booth to discuss philosophy, especially Gurdjieff, Sartre and Ouspensky. We talked about the zen of shoveling shit and other unpleasant and hard labor. And the quest for the perfect moment, always destroyed before realized, usually ruined by well-doers. Also, the analysis of language and its absurdity—"Seat.

Somebody named that Seat." To which Sue exclaimed, "Yeah, so somebody named that 'seat,' get over it and get on with your life."

I was always embarrassed by the names of our restaurant's offerings: the Cock-a-Doodle-Doo Olé, the Atilla the Ham, the Ike and Tina Tuna...

The place fell on difficult times. There were frequent and extreme shortages. We would open for brunch without eggs. Our paychecks often could not be cashed due to lack of funds. As employees in such trying circumstances, we began to fight among ourselves. Continually, creditors came and demanded payment; we had nothing to give them. The manager those days made himself scarce.

We were out of three quarters of the items on the menu. We were also deluged with customers. Kay, Rob, Peter and I were the only staff. I began to get so stressed that life began to seem like watching a movie. Cutting insults were exchanged. Rob insulted my ability to cook. Peter and Kay nearly came to blows over the fact that she was using too many pots and pans. I ended up yelling at Rob. Then we realized that we weren't the problem. Finally, Rob walked into the dining room and said, "Ladies and gentlemen, drop your forks. You don't have to pay for your meals. Just get out!"

Confused, and slowly, the roomful of customers left.

We called the owner, turned off the ovens and locked the doors.

On the way home, we stopped for beer at a little pub called Baggin's End, then ice cream cones with coffee back from McDonald's. We were carefree — we always seemed to manage rent.

12

A MAP OF FLOWERING TREES

It amazed me, the stencils painted on the sidewalks of my neighborhood:

A WOMAN WAS RAPED HERE
A WOMAN WAS RAPED HERE

One just outside my door. Again on my way to the bakery. There again by the coffee shop. All over.

Sue and I refused to give into oppression. We made a list of the flowering pink and white trees in the neighborhood and converted this information into a map.

Sex could never destroy me. I had been a prostitute, been raped—date rape was, for a piece of my history, almost an expectation. I cared not at all. Searching my deepest depths for them, I could find no wounds, no scars, just "Oh, well. Men are scum."

One evening Kay and I were, in coveted Blondie's words, "standing on a corner with a piece of pizza." Some kind gent had given us slices of his pie; he said he had too much. We relished the chance to act out one of our favorite songs. Until some yokels came out of a bar across the street (where I had sometimes sought refuge from potential rapists), drunkenly yelling something about our sexuality—"fucking lesbians!" or some such weak little would-be insult. As they jeered on in this pesky though still threatening manner, a friend of ours happed along. John returned the sentiment to them, questioning their sexuality. (His remark,though unremembered, was much more original and witty than theirs.) The largest of them walked across the street to where we were standing; we all expected further verbiage. Without a pause, this man knocked John several feet to the concrete. Everything happening so quickly, it was serendipity that more of our ranks arrived; for a short time, a battle ensued with fists flying and a knife made its appearance—a very dangerous situation until police sirens emptied the streets. We refuged at Kay's nearby apartment.

The rubber shark in Kay's refrigerator was set to spring forth upon the opening of the door. She frequently sent unsuspecting folk on missions therein, hoping, wildly, to frighten them. But the only one she succeeded in scaring was herself, and that was almost every time she opened the door. Also in her booby-trapped apartment was the killer chair that would dump whoever happened to lean back in it, arms a-flailing; again the only victims were Kay and me.

Living as a cheap hooker, my main drink was cheap vodka with "Purplesaurus Rex" Kool-Aid. Kay tossed back Café Lolitas with cream. These drinks were of a better quality than our previous Mad Dog or gin-and-Tab. Our daily repast included canned chili, packaged macaroni with powdered cheese, and either Oreos in milk or dry Cap'n Crunch with Crunchberries.

I fell in love with two men sharing an apartment in the building across the alley from Kay's apartment. I spied on them incessantly, and we sometimes had conversations or exchanged remarks. They were fairly recently freed from the state prison (I think for armed robbery). My favorite of the two was working as a baker in a cheap pie shop. Their motorcycles (parked in the alley) sounded the alarm on their comings and goings.

We watched with small binoculars and vigorous joy, through their uncurtained windows, as they pumped away on girls we hoped were their girlfriends. Until Kay gave us away by loudly squealing.

I visited them one night and (this I should have suspected from previous conversations) they forced sex on me. This ordeal lasted over two hours. I was upset to be hit with some kind of martial arts weapon, my arms and back were bruised, but my major complaint was that they made me spit out my coconut Life Savers (there were only two in a roll). Bastards!

As I left, I realized there was a cherry tree growing in front of their building.

13

A LITTLE NIGHT MUSIC

I had been conversing plainly and lewdly with and lap dancing upon two men—Dante and Truman. I wanted to dance, but since there was no dance floor, I tried to enjoy the overtly sexual conversation while mimicking it in dance upon and around them. Our sexual discourse spanned an hour. They were especially interested in positions and my responses; they weren't interested in talking about their own gratification. They left the bar with me. Okay, I was loud—I got us kicked out of the bar.

We went to a parked Jaguar and soon were speeding down the highway, past the lighted billboards and a huge sign reminding me that I am a Sinner. The conversation continued. The house we parked at was in the hills; it was a very tasteful estate. They laid me on the floor. I succumbed to their desires.

They removed my clothing, piece by piece. They positioned my body in various poses. They stroked and manipulated me on the teal green rug. They placed burning candles all around me. Dante put on Lou Reed's "Berlin" record. Appropriately melancholy in action and atmosphere. I listened to the familiar songs about suicides and traumatized children as Truman oversaw and corrected Dante's touches, erogenous though not rawly sexual.

They didn't want me to touch them or even see their bodies — only exposing their heads and their hands. I gained nothing apart from an unusual experience in my cap. It indeed appealed to my sense of the strange.

Later, my strange experiences continued:

"I'm looking for a good time," said this man at my bus stop.

"Want to get a drink?" he went on.

In that annoy-myself mood, I affirmed. We took a city bus to The Alibi. The bartender put salt on the rim of my blended strawberry margarita — ugh! We didn't stay long.

The neighborhood the bus dropped us off at what looked like a scene from a brutal war. His house was rundown but acceptable. He kissed me. He fried up a mess o' hog jowls; I've never been sure, but I think it was supposed to be an aphrodisiac. "Strange," I thought, it tasted like bacon. Also puzzling, we engaged in a precoital game of chess. I won — unusual.

Deep into our consummation of the relationship, we were interrupted by his roommate. Seeping into yet more sleaze, I let him join in for a bit until I salvaged some self-respect and, it being near dawn, took the bus home.

14

HE IS THE EGG MAN

Kay tried several means of employment. Her geisha work was impeded by her looking, they said, like a school marm or a drag queen by turns. But she liked pouring out sake, lighting cigarettes, initiating and engaging in eclectic conversation and mostly looking pretty. Those were Kay's favorite and most doable jobs, the ones where all she had to do was look pretty.

She tried modeling, first in an art class — sometimes nude, sometimes in striking outfits. But true to her form, there were mishaps — once the skirt she was wearing fell off; she was thinking how she liked the length better than she remembered, then it slipped to the floor. She was naked from the waist down — oh, well, embarrassing, but at least it was just the art class.

One job she found most remarkable and not altogether uncomfortable. Her job title was Assistant, though she had no idea what that would entail. As it turned out, she was supposed to feast on eggs while her employer massaged her feet. She had only one large helping of eggs (though that part was integral). Scrambled. But the older man massaged her feet for hours. She wondered if she should do something else and then insisted on it. So the man gave her fifty dollars and sent her to go buy him some paper from the stationery store down the street. She entertained the notion that she could keep the fifty and call it over between her and the egg man. But she bought the paper and diligently brought back the correct amount of change. In the end, she was given a hundred dollars. She wondered if she should go back for more eggs and massage another day; though despite the attractiveness of novelty, she felt it was kind of creepy.

She towered over her new beau. People would say, "kinky sex," as they walked by, blissfully holding hands. He wore a suit, she looked more like a punk rocker. She tall, he not so much. He was a playwright and a reader of Polish literature. (She remembered particularly him reading aloud to her about a talking mulch and a renowned professor of Synthesis chasing a red balloon.) She ate pints of mocha ice cream and watched *The A-Team* on a small black and white TV. He made her work. So she did; she got a job in a department store spraying innocent passersby with expensive perfumes, hoarding small sample vials for herself and her friends.

She preferred the job of hotel maid, where she could feast, sometimes serendipitously, on discarded room-service meals and watch soap operas. There was never anyone to watch over her work. Her favorite rooms were the ones that had "Do Not Disturb" signs on the doors or people who wanted only clean towels.

She was called "Lips" by her male workmates because of her dark lipstick. And she ate alone (not always by choice) in the company lunchroom.

She just wanted to be taken care of.

15

ROOMS IN SHANGHAI

Around midnight the drag queens started to displace the Middle Eastern students. The all-night restaurant served fairly good and plentiful coffee, spooned into our mouths and mixed with pourings of cream and fake sugar, and for food, a Tapioca Royale (the only thing affordable).

The students always suspected that Kay and I were lovers. On more than one occasion, they sought to have group sex with us. They sent, by way of the busboy, a note written on a napkin: "We know you are lisbeens. But we will pay anything you want." They claimed to have much wealth, yet their offers were never generous enough to entice us. It was always interesting though, to watch lustful men making their attempts at seduction; it bore the fruit of laughter.

Once when we asked the waiter for water, he left, then returned to ask if we wanted it in a glass.

We'd sit in our booth, talking all night, frequently stoned on something (often LSD—my favorite). I had once been a Mexican, once a popular late night talk show host, and once I was convinced I was a tampon. In the morn, psychotically tired and with acid hangovers, we would "tingle with terrible tiredness"—Kay's description. And our acid personae would fade away.

Often of an evening, we would make the trek up to QP's for our nightly joe, ladled into our mouths from ceramic mugs with teaspoons. We endured snow or ice or sweltering heat or sudden downpour—we braved all alike.

With Neal one afternoon, we suddenly realized that we could call everything "room" (pronounced with a French accent):

"Beautiful room today!"

"The room is shining, not a room in the sky."

"Could you run grab me a room?" and so forth…

One night with Neal, in Sue's bedroom: "Shanghai is in China?" he asked.

Obviously he bore no relation to my father, whose car travel entertainment consisted of:

"Leningrad!"

Answered by: "Sixty north, thirty east."

Then: "Urumqi!"

"Eighty-eight east, forty-eight north."

Ignorance of geography was a defect worthy of excommunication. So Neal was dismissed from the family, obviously; though cute and Latvian, he was no longer boyfriend material.

I bought a little rabbit at this time; a dwarf rabbit whose name was, of course, Room. He was very sweet and, trained in the ways of bodily functions, he could run around my apartment freely. Then he began to chew wires, destroying, in succession, a record player and an alarm clock. I was always late for work. I had to keep him caged while I was out. I'd become involved with a man and I was rarely home. Room died of loneliness and confinement; I'm sure of this. I would always blame myself for his death.

Late one night, I bought a peapod at the neighborhood grocery. I was charged a nickel—an exorbitant price, I thought.

On the way home, I let my attention stray a bit and so did not see that I was on a collision course with a towering, scruffy man with noticeably crazed eyes and wild, abundant hair.

"Oh, excuse me," I said, trying to remain unruffled.

"Will you marry me in heaven?"

I noticed a knife. "Oops," I thought, "faux pas."

"I don't really know you enough for that." Again striving for calm.

"Come with me to heaven!"

I tried to steer his mind from the idea of heaven.

"How about if I meet you in the park tomorrow?" I said, trying to be resourceful.

"You've got nice titties too, not like a hound's ears."

I inched my way toward the door of an open bar. "Well, I'll see you tomorrow!"

"You've made me so happy!" he exclaimed.

I ducked into the bar. Glad to have kept my wits about me. Resolved to better watch where I was going.

And of course, afraid that I might encounter "Hound's Ears" (as he came to be known) again.

A bevy of bikers moved into my building. I was intimidated; I thought they would hate me. One day, I got into a conversation with one regarding whether or not he should "go kill someone." He calmed down, then said, "You're pretty god-damned weird! You must get a lot of shit too."

"Indeed, I do," I acknowledged.

"If anyone is ever harassing you, just let me know." A promise he and his friends kept.

While racing up the stairs one night to quickly make mac and cheese before our movie came on — Kay had the TV in her place, I had the stove in mine — the biker jumped out of his open door and yelled, "Is there someone after you?! Are you okay?!" We reassured him, as he assured us of our safety.

On one occasion, I was walking home from work (swing shift), and as I walked down the deserted street next to a dangerous park, I saw a man walking with a bundle of helium filled balloons. He walked toward me; a little nervous, I walked faster. He hastened his step too. I finally started to run and he chased me. He let the balloons go and ran quickly. I managed to get to the bar where my biker friends were drinking. They ran out to catch the balloon man, but he had faded into the night.

A MEMORY OF THE OCEAN

Before our next major trip overseas, we packed ourselves away to one of the most favored venues in our
world—the ocean—to say good-bye for a time, we
didn't know for how long.

The heightened awe we felt that afternoon, perhaps, had something to do with our next day's trip to
foreign climes. Whatever it was, we were mesmerized.
The ocean that day seemed especially powerful; it was
the God I used to pray to. There were piles of sand
boulders—lifting them made you look like a super-
hero, but they were feather light. We tossed them about
and crushed them in our hands. For an afternoon, we
didn't want to go to Europe. We wanted to stay at this
beach; we wanted to be the sun-drenched sand, the
seagulls gliding over the waves. We wanted to be on
the last bit of land before an infinite, all-mighty power.
Facing one way—endless water. The other way—an
entire continent.

The waves came rolling in from diverse, remote
lands; it looked like the bounds of the world. Evergreen
trees, shaped by centuries of constant winds, marched
down tall, rolling mountains, then stopped suddenly at

the precipices of sandy cliffs. The beaches were interrupted at intervals by great, craggy rocks. To get to the beach, it was necessary to wind your way down a narrow trail etched into the cliffs. It was pristine. It was lonely. With the tide pools and caves, it was magical.

We spotted in tide pools sea tarantulas doing battle, and sea stars, and brightly colored anemones. We tried to lose ourselves in the high rocks. It was a glorious, clear day—perfect for enjoying this stretch of coastline. We had traveled for hours, journeying from the furious reality of the city to these enrapturing surroundings.

We walked and ran and splashed in the icy tide. We ran away from swift-advancing waves, then turned and ran into them. We sought out caves that stretched to deepness—"doing battle," we said of them, "like the sea tarantulas." Down the beach ran a pack of wild dogs. We breathed the sea salt. Kay and I searched for perfect, powerful ocean rocks to be kept as prevention from ills. (But, as my Dad had warned me when I was a kid, possibly spiritually too heavy.)

Engaged in this pursuit, it surprised us a bit when we noticed a man walking down the beach. He was wearing a medieval prince's clothing. We were sure he must be from some previous time, some glorious land. The wild dogs ran around him and seagulls circled his head. He was heading for a cave (doing battle) that we hadn't seen before. We jumped. Of course! That cave was a magical time-and-place machine of some sort.

We had to catch him before he disappeared, we'd beg him to take us along. We ran. We ran so that I couldn't feel my legs anymore and my breath seemed to be on fire. We had to catch that prince. We were tired of our mundane day-to-day existence, in the mood for more magic.

As we drew close, we saw that the prince was a middle-aged, bearded man in denim cutoffs and a shirt bearing the Nike logo, common, definitely present day. The dogs were just his pets, and the cave just a slight indentation in the cliffs.

Life dragged for two long days after this letdown. Then, Europe.

17

ANARCHY IN EUROPE

We desperately wanted to marry and to live in Europe. We also craved adventure. The fun we'd had before this was nothing to what we hoped would come to pass. We were most hopeful of meeting up with international drug smugglers or spies. The smugglers, it turned out, were not hard to find.

Once again Kay and I frugally saved and flew standby. Once again we brought far too little money for our needs.

Our anarchic trip through Europe lasted just six months. At first we traveled by train and slept in rented rooms. But that came to an end fairly soon due to lack of funds. So the trip was furthered by hitchhiking and staying with people we met, remarkable or not. We were continually certain that we were going to die on the streets; we were never entirely pleased that we hadn't.

We both tried to trust completely that fate would provide. We had little care about where we were going—often we did not know. We never despaired; we looked for opportunities that would work for the moment.

I had landed in London three days before Kay due to the bad planning of standby tickets. I was surprised on arrival by the very lax customs agents; all they did was stamp a six-month visa into my passport without question or comment. I exchanged some money there. I took notice of the peculiar purple toilet paper in the women's room—pretty, but crackly and not very absorbent. (Later on, I'd be forced to use ripped-out pages of *Paris Match*.) I was bewildered at not being able to find the exit. I wandered for a while, occasionally seeing signs that said "Way Out." These I paid no attention to, other than to remember The Flintstones' concert with The Way Outs: "Here come the Way Outs… Way out!" I was searching for "Exit." Then, of course! *Way Out!*

I found myself taking the underground to Earl's Court. It sounded good, not having any idea where to go. I came to Holland Park, where I sat. Then I ventured to Bayswater, realizing I had to do something about lodgings. I sat for another hour. I bought a croissant from a small store. The cashier directing me to Pembroke Lane, where I did find a room at last, just as the evening advanced.

The next day, I sat in lovely Kensington Gardens. A black man approached me and we fell to talking. I was in love with his accent; he was from Barbados. We went for coffee, I was glad for a companion. His apartment yielded original works of very fine art, some of which were his own creations. We ate eggs scrambled in rice. We passed an enrapturing night. The next day I said good-bye, by which I meant finally, though I was supposed to meet him later.

When Kay arrived, we had to search for a new hotel, as mine was too small and more expensive than we could afford. She, in desperation, flagged down a car. I thought the driver would be mad that she had yelled at him.

"This is your doing. I'll have none of it." I took some steps away.

Yet the man, Robert, was not angry at all. He asked what we needed. We offered to be his live-in cook and maid. He told us to wait while he got rid of his dogs (two large Dobermans). We waited, giggling and exclaiming, excited that we were in for adventure, both sure he wouldn't return. He did.

"Where are you from?" he asked.

"The States."

"I realize that." He continued, "Where in the States?"

"Oregon, Portland."

I wasn't surprised at the time, yet in looking back he was one of about four people we met in Europe with whom this same conversation didn't go:

"Where are you from?"

"West Coast."

"California?"

"No, Oregon."

"Oregon, California?"

"No, just Oregon. It's a state between California and Washington."

"Washington is on the East Coast."

"California." Defeated.

Robert took us to a charming small bed-and-breakfast—The Sevan, close to Hyde Park. He ensconced us in a room with a bed for each, a shower in the room (unusual for Europe) and a television (also unusual), though it only had two stations; our first night we had the choice of a ball game or a kidney operation.

"What line o' work are you in?" Kay asked.

"I'm a commodities dealer," he answered.

"What kind of commodities?" we both wondered.

"Whatever is in demand," the reply came smooth, yet with the beginnings of irritation.

"Like plastic barrels?" Kay asked.

"No," he said, seeming to wonder at our naiveté.

"Why not?" Curious.

"Because they're not in demand!" Clearly wanting to change the subject.

"What if they were?" I asked.

"If plastic barrels achieve great popularity, I'll consider dealing in them," stated such that there was no question that the subject was now closed.

After Robert went home for the evening, Kay and I decided to explore. We sought out a pub. There I had my first taste of Pernod; I liked it very much (though later I would prefer ouzo).

We came across a cinema featuring the unabridged version of *Caligula*. In we went. I found it most entertaining, though I was glad to be seeing it with Kay, rather than someone I knew less, or especially a man (be he date or otherwise).

Robert had sex with me in our room, but he was in love with Kay. He took her with him to a warehouse; a few people were doing various duties. He showed her diamonds, put them in her hands—made clear the description of "commodities dealer." She was intrigued, quite so, but she was grappling with a persistent, new problem of being unable to have sex for gain more than for love.

We stayed up all night, concocting schemes whereby she might escape the entire sex issue. But there was no way to postpone it forever. We waited at the hotel for him the next day. That day he was going to take us to his house in Devon. He was always about an hour late, yet when he didn't show up by the appointed hour of noon, we left. Relieved, though never to be sure what that path had in store.

The greatest fun began the day we departed our landing port of London. We began a frenzy of travel that often enough left us not realizing where we were. "If it's Tuesday, this must be…"

Never the sort to be considered tourists, we often encountered, by accident, works that we had read about in school. On encountering *Manneken Pis* in Brussels or the golden mermaid looking out to sea from Copenhagen, I always thought, "Oh, so that's where that is."

However, when we took the train to Paris from Brussels (Gauloises cigarettes were cheaper there), we found that for some reason Paris brought out the tourists in us that no other city had. We climbed the steps to Sacré-Coeur in Montmartre, beautiful in architecture and flowers. We walked the length of the Champs-Élysées—I was surprised to find a McDonald's there and an Aeroflot office. We walked to the Arc de Triomphe. We had our pictures taken in front of the Eiffel Tower and we boated down the Seine.

The truly wonderful aspect of our travels was the complete freedom. There were no schedules, nothing that had to be done. We stayed in a place until we got bored, then we just picked another place and resumed hitchhiking, which brought its own adventure often enough.

Our first trip to the continent was on a stormy day; we were thrilled that we would soon be in Amsterdam—the destination to which we had always had the hope that some madman would fling us free tickets. The daylight was diminishing as we left, and it didn't seem very long until we landed in Harwich; the ferry waited. Having not a very solid grasp on geography, the space on the map we thought was quite small, we assumed that the ship would dock in an hour or two. We waited in the bar. On Kay's questioning, they laughed at our ignorance; the ship wouldn't dock for another eight or so hours.

We went out on the deck besieged with storm. There was, naturally, no one about. We danced up and down; we danced furiously and happily to Kay's taped Kiss music—"I was Made for Loving You Baby." We were going to Amsterdam! The rocking waves and powerful winds made us all the more delirious. We got soaked. We were living a dream.

Holland had not the amount of windmills that I thought it should, and we had just missed any possible tulip sightings due to the recently changed season. But Amsterdam was glorious. Everyone (it seemed) rode bicycles. And people gave you directions using canals instead of streets—"Oh, yes, that's three canals down then five to the right." Then there was the night revelry. And revel we did!

There was, of course, a man. Moustapha from Morocco. He spoke excellent English. He loved "The Muppet Show" and pointed out just the same things that Kay and I also liked. He wanted to take us to Morocco, where he said we could relax in the sun and pluck fresh figs and grapes. I liked him, yet for some reason I found sex with him repugnant—an uncommon predicament for me; always before I had been able to put up with much more to further my goals. The day I left him, he chased us down the street trying to press his phone number into my hand; Kay took it, baffled by my actions but because of my disgust, we never saw him again.

Some English youths, in their thick accents, told Kay, "You look like Tuba Carmen."

"Tuba Carmen?" Kay enunciated back.

"Yeah, Tuba Carmen."

"Who the Jesus is Tuba Carmen?"

"Tuba Carmen," they said, and one moved his arms in the stereotypical Egyptian way. "Tuba Carmen."

"You mean Tutankhamen!" we clarified, amazed.

"Yeah," they said. Could they not hear the difference?

"Funny you should say that," Kay said, "because I am!"

We'd often mimicked the boy king. But beyond that, I could never see the resemblance.

18

DEFINED BY GUM

I've never felt culture shock. I think if you can just relax and resist having to understand everything, you'll fit in physically and mentally.

So it was that no one ever believed we were Americans. In a square in Amsterdam, a man once approached us with a request in his own language.

"Do you speak English?" I asked.

"Where are you from?" he responded.

"The States."

"No, you're not," derisively.

"Actually, I am." I wondered why someone would pretend to be from the States if they weren't; I didn't find it a source of pride.

"Oh, no. The only thing American about you is the way you chew your gum!"

Instead of expensive and questionable restaurant meals (the escargots had feelers and suction cups, and the shrimp came with head, feet and an unappetizing vein), we shopped in the little bakeries and produce markets and dairies. We almost never ate anything except bread and cheese and candy. We liked to sit in parks or on subway stairs and eat. We grew to love Chipitos and paprika chips and the grey, colorless would-be Starbursts — Sugus.

We drenched ourselves in fountains and contemplated throwing everything we owned into a canal and spending all our money on the kind of vacuum cleaners that have a long hose and a body that drags behind — a cannister model, I believe — and living out our lives in Iran, where, at the time, Americans were pretty much illegal. We thought that if we could annoy ourselves as fully as that, we would have reached the nirvana of irritation, so we'd be freed up. But we didn't.

Instead, we decided it was time to leave, see other sights. We just brainstormed interesting places to visit and decided on Venice. The train took us through Germany. We were at the border when I realized that I had a chunk of hashish that was given to us gratis by a fellow American in our favorite Amsterdam square. The woman in our cabin remarked that they sometimes brought dogs on the trains to search for drugs. I held up the hash and mouthed to Kay, "What am I going to do with this?" Almost instantly the German customs agent appeared. "Do you have any drugs?" Kay and I sat with the hash sandwiched securely between us. "Drugs? No. I don't have any drugs. Have you got drugs, Kay?" "No. No drugs." He stared at us for long minutes, then asked, "What about weapons?" I think Kay saved us by retrieving some oranges and innocently admitting, "We have some fruit."

The Italian customs, however, laughed a lot and patted our behinds. I don't think they would have cared if we had sat there smoking hash. They most likely would have joined us.

The beach at Lido was unique to me. The water was so lightly bluish-green, the gleaming white sand strewn with fragile shells that I had never before seen except in gift shops. It was the first time I had swum in warm salt water. I ignored the prominent, obvious warning sign, since my Italian was limited to "benissimo... mangiare... cappuccino..." And I was having a splendid day. I was pulled away from the beach by a strong wave and exhausted myself trying to get back to shore. No one noticed my struggling; I was too embarrassed to call out. I was just becoming afraid when the wave let me loose. I made it to shore and never again swam at Lido.

But I did have sex there before I left, behind a sand dune, with a Venetian glass blower I met in a little bar near the beach. I showered to wash away the traces and left.

19

FUN WITH STORMS

We attempted to squeeze between the guards lining the square, but they offered us no passage. President Carter was in town and they were taking precautions for that. We waited until he left, catching a glimpse of him boarding a police boat. Except for walking, there's no other transportation besides boats in Venice.

The guards relaxed and joked with us for a minute. Then, in typical Italian form, one of them decided to quit for the day; he treated Kay and me to gelato. We had no language in common; we gestured a lot. He tried to explain his job to us.

"You're the King of Italy!" I announced.

"Oh! You defend the King of Italy," Kay had deduced.

Together we chimed, "Is there a King of Italy?"

He gave up.

In hopes of a contribution, we only slightly down-played our financial situation—it was bleak. He told us to come with him. We thought we were walking to a hotel. He brought us to a police station; he thought we needed money to return to the States. We just wanted to have fun.

As we walked back toward our hotel, it began to rain. It rained harder and harder. Then the sky lit up with flashes of the colorless noon of untamed electricity. The city's power went out. Running now, a defeated attempt to keep from getting soaked. A moment of complete darkness, then again, a brief flash, as we tripped our way over canal bridges' oddly spaced stairs. Tourists gathered under shelters, singing, "You are my sunshine…"

At last we found our hotel. The shutters were closed against the storm. There was one sole candle lit in the dim lobby. Inside, the desk clerk was entertaining two friends. Kay and I stormed in and we all fell to talking, again with the language barrier. One friend went for wine; he came back with one bottle.

"Are you insane?" I wondered vehemently. "That's a pittance!"

He asked how many bottles I could drink. I made a rough guess—nine.

So he ran next door for eight more—all red (though I've forgotten which varietal). We drank with stupor as the goal. Before that occurred, I asked the desk clerk to choke me to death. Sure that I was joking, he wrapped his hands around my neck. A little squeeze, then a little harder, just starting to become painful—he was waiting for my "Uncle!"

It did not come. He fell back all at once, realizing that I was serious, most serious, dead serious. Finding something very wrong in my mental state, they retreated. But I lay on the floor, drinking for hours.

The next day, we checked out. We wanted to go to Germany. As funds were limited, we wanted the cheapest passage, though with no notion of geography, we asked:

"How much is a ticket to Hamburg?" The answer too high. We stepped away from the ticket booth to discuss.

"How much to Frankfurt?" Again too high, more discussion.

"We'll take the cheapest ticket to Germany." He booked us. We started to walk away again.

"Oh! Where are we going?" we had to ask.

"Munich."

Dread. We bought the tickets. We had once more started to walk away. Then, "Oh! When does the train leave?" Mystifed by us, the clerk started to become annoyed.

We shared the train's compartment with an exaltation of nuns. They were quite friendly and dressed as nuns should, in beautiful habits.

20

TEUFEL ODER AXTMÖRDER

Munich. I remember all the shops full of Peltze—furs. At the time I wanted one; now the thought sickens me. I thought about how my German language classes had been a waste; I could not understand this language. But when we heard a couple from Hamburg, I realized that it was Bavarian I didn't understand; High German had indeed been pretty much mastered.

"Gimmer," we were told instead of "Gehen wir." "Iau" meant "ich auch," and on…

We were kicked out of our hotel one day because in the previous wee hours I had screamed most alarmedly when a spider crawled on me. It caused quite some commotion, though I'm sure in the States it would not have been even a cause for remark.

We met up with two Greek men, Andre and Bobby. Unfortunately, I was coupled with Bobby. He pretended to have great wealth, though in actuality he was living on Andre's good graces.

The first night was all right, pre-wrath-of-Bobby—though both Kay and I bled all over our beds—oops! Social blunder. Faux pas. And ironically, it wasn't either of our times. As we crept down to the restroom to clean up, Kay broke the key off in the door. This provoked gales of laughter from me and then her. Thankfully, someone came to our aid — they just stuck the key stump back in the lock and voila! It latched again.

Unbeknownst to her, Kay became engaged to Andre. He was very serious, she oblivious. She was, at this time, going through a period of what must have been stress-induced psychosis. She would sit for hours and chuckle to herself. She repeated ad infinitum, "Ich bin der Teufel. Ich bin auch ein Axtmörder." (I am the devil. I am also an axe murderer.) Though this was just something we liked to exclaim when overwhelmed or excited. Andre's family members (he lived with his mother and father, brother and his wife and their developmentally disabled child) and I would talk and drink Scotch at all hours. Kay would sit babbling in the corner, convinced that everyone was saying "Teufel" to her and that we were trying to drive her mad by making the lights constantly dim and brighten.

She criticized my musical ability when I began to sing the "Ich bin der Teufel" song I composed, jumping in mid-song to say the end note was a musical error or something. But she hadn't heard the end, which then set her straight.

Bobby became evil. He threatened to cut my face up if I didn't satisfy him. Andre said only, "Bobby ist bose." (Bobby is mad/bad.) This phrase stuck with us; we often said a caricatured impression of it to amuse ourselves. But at the time I was scared. He finally left, or rather Andre made him go.

We met a Turkish man; he fell in love with Kay. It was not reciprocated.

"Why doesn't she like me?" Uchel asked. "I have good shoulders."

The reason was obvious; continually from the first night of our meeting, he had slobbered all over her, wailing, "My California queen!"

I still believed there was an opportunity there that Kay was missing. He had a diamond watch; he drove a BMW. He took us to a Turkish restaurant owned by friends of his; one of the owners went on a mission to find me some American cigarettes. They brought out special, cushioned chairs for us to sit in and made all the food and drink selections.

Kay tried to like Uchel. Her lip was bruised from kissing, but she preferred Andre.

We tried to get work visas, but we were not successful. We were offered under-the-counter jobs as lures in a small bar—like German Geishas. We were paid to get men to run up huge bills and want to return. I sat with them, lighting their cigarettes, pouring drinks for them, keeping them amused. It was harder than I thought it would be, keeping lulls from occurring and anticipating others' wants.

Kay and I knew we had to travel on. We cried with Andre. A song on the radio about Amsterdam for some reason made the job of leaving harder. He tore a page from his atlas—Germany—and gave it to us. It was in Greek, but oh, well. He insisted that we not go through East Germany—he didn't trust us, we kind of drew trouble. We were headed to Scandinavia, ultimately to Sweden to stay with my pen pal of the last few years. With the little money we had made working, we abandoned the train in favor of the less expensive hitchhiking.

The rest stops had vending machines: raw ground-beef sandwiches, sausages, beer.

"Obst und Gemusse, immer Frisch aus Italien," (Fruit and Vegetables, always Fresh from Italy) said the truck that took us to Hamburg. The driver feasted us with fruit from his cargo, luscious peaches and plums and a ripe mango. It was humorous to hear German CB radio language; this on the heels of the American craze. The German forest from our view was thin and scraggly, though we didn't venture from the Autobahn.

We slept the night in the truck, and in the morn set out to discover Hamburg. We didn't stay very long.

I remember a horrifying elevator. It consisted of many wooden boxes stacked upon each other; they were in perpetual motion and one must hop on and off at the right moment. Once on, you were plunged frightfully into blinding blackness, very disorienting. We clung to each other and couldn't wait to hop off.

We stopped at a Burger King where I haltingly tried to order fast food in German. The cashier let me struggle and when I finished, he repeated it all back in

English. Thanks.

We took the ferry from Puttgarden to Rodby—a short distance; we were in Denmark. We met up with an Englishman who was seeing how far north he could get on his holidays. We all sat for hours on a curb. Finally a very small and already crowded car stopped; the Englishman bid us go. We were sorry to leave him behind, yet glad of a ride—this one all the way to Copenhagen!

We were dropped off at the train station, there we could book a cheap hotel. We did—The Viking (how original). But it was sufficient and clean. Somehow, we later discovered, reaching over the counter at night to retrieve our keys, Kay had been checked in as "Stormer Stanner." For years after, her friends would call her Stormy.

In the morning, the fare for the breaking of the fast was most excellent. With no money to speak of, we stuffed our pockets with rolls and cheese for lunch.

We got cake from Hare Krishnas as we explored around. Finally, after we had fruitlessly tried to sneak in, two men bought our way into Tivoli Gardens. Beautiful! Circus acts and fun rides, lovely cafes and fireworks at night.

We met our first Swedes in the public square. We exuded our only Swedish: "Kan vi hyra golfklubbar?" They didn't understand the context and exclaimed with their accents, "Klubber?" From then on we would exclaim "Klubber" when perplexed or surprised.

We came across some shabby looking men who asked us if we wanted to go to the Rosa Luxembourg Café. We had never heard the name before; without much thought, we agreed. For some reason, on that particular day, we were dressed in peculiarly American clothes—myself in "I Heart Oregon" shorts, Kay a Coca-Cola tee shirt, and we were both wearing Nike tennis shoes. It was a dark basement kind of pub, filled with smoke. We walked in chattering, oblivious. We sat down at a table. Then I noticed we were attracting many stares, though no hostility. I definitely felt out of place, especially when I looked at the wall above me and saw a giant American flag with swastikas instead of stars. I diverted my eyes only to notice on another wall, an American Indian with tears on his face. We didn't stay long.

Another unexpected turn—two Danish youths accosted us and drove us away for being American.

In Sweden, we met a couple of locals at a café in the town of Falkenberg. It was a beautiful café, tables outdoors on a grassy slope. There we made the acquaintance of Oleg—who would be my pen pal of many years.

We spent our days mostly sunning our buttocks at the (rather filthy) beach. There, for the first time we came across fast food mashed potatoes. The fellow eating them we would refer to as "Tate." We listened to The Beach Boys and ABBA.

Oleg and his friends took us to a nightclub, but we didn't dance—not just there, we never danced much in public anymore. But Oleg danced ridiculously and remarkably (not good). And we didn't like the way he held his loaded fork in midair when speaking.

But eventually they dropped us at a good vantage point for hitchhiking and I had no further contact with him.

21

INTERNATIONAL DRUG SMUGGLERS
OR SPIES?

It was getting late to be hitchhiking. The sun had set long since and it was starting to get cold. The highway just outside Copenhagen was beginning to offer fewer and fewer opportunities. Kay and I didn't care. Even though we were somewhat stranded, we were having great fun occupying ourselves doing imitations of Swedes riding go-carts.

Thoroughly engaged in our rather silly activity, we were a little surprised when a car indeed finally stopped. It was a brand new, bright blue Mazda with a Norwegian registry — a little odd in the usual sea of blandly colored, mostly German models. Two attractive, young men stepped out to help us with our bags. We were a little intrigued that the car's trunk was already half-full with rich fur coats. With all packed, Kay and I slid into the comfortable back seat.

The men introduced themselves as Ben and Mike. In response to my request for cigarettes, Mike asked, "Regular, menthol, filtered or straight?"

Kay and I exchanged looks; maybe we were in for a spell of luck.

They apologized for the lack of music and said they were having a stereo installed the next day. It was only then that they inquired where we were going; somehow this usually important question hadn't concerned any of us. And in fact, Kay and I didn't really care; we had a vague plan to check out Greece. But we said a little tentatively, "Berlin"; it would be a good first stop.

Ben replied that they were heading for Amsterdam. He enthusiastically invited us to come with. Kay and I loved Amsterdam; more than that, we loved adventure, and this was already shaping up to be quite fun.

We drove on through the night; Ben and Mike conversed in Danish.

It wasn't very long before we came to water and had to board a ferry to Fyn. We parked the car and started for the ship's restaurant. Ben asked if we were hungry; we replied sheepishly that we had no money.

"I didn't ask you if you had money. I asked you if you wanted something to eat."

Kay and I were very pleased, both at Ben's elegance and also for the opportunity to sate our growing hunger. We dined and drank and conversed quite freely, and it didn't seem long until the ship docked.

We drove on again, heading for Odense, but after a while, as we were all tired, we stopped at a hotel—The Brazilia. The men went in and paid for two rooms; we all went into one. Ben asked if we liked it—we did; it was much nicer than lodgings we'd had in some time. The men left. Kay and I were a little curious but quite happy—why were there no strings attached? We wondered about the furs and what would happen in Amsterdam. Who were these men? What fun! Maybe this was our coveted chance to be Bonnie and Clyde!

We tried to sleep, but outside our window it sounded like some monstrous, scary boar was emoting loudly all night.

In the morning a fine breakfast was brought to our room—rolls with butter, cheese and ham, and lots of coffee with fresh cream and of course, little bottles of Stoli. Kay flooded the bathroom, attempting to use what was actually just a shower head aimed at a drain in the floor. The maid appeared as the water was just spilling into the rest of the room. We got in trouble and I didn't get to shower. The men promptly appeared, and we eagerly returned to the highway.

The Danish countryside yielded lovely little villages with houses with thatched roofs and sprinkled with castle-esque churches; the land was pretty flat but nicely green. There were fields aplenty with grazing dairy cattle and strangely bundled hay.

We finally stopped. We had coffee and broodjes while we waited for the stereo installation. Mike turned and asked, "Can you do the clean machine?" He moved his arm up and down to illustrate.

"Yeah, it's a nice car," Kay replied, thinking that he must be referring to the new car we were riding in. At the same time I said, "No, we don't dance," thinking he must be referring to the latest moves.

It took a while, but we discovered that he was asking us to vacuum.

Kay and I had come complete with cassette tapes, so at last we didn't want for a soundtrack to brighten our adventure. And we glided down the highway—drink in one hand, cigarette in the other, as Blondie issued forth from the stereo.

Odense was nice. We visited Hans Christian Andersen's garden. It had a statue of Yul Brynner (Kay and I were very gullible—but it was a remarkable resemblance).

For some reason, we had to go to a hardware store. We thought better of asking why. Kay and I sought out the axes; she wielded one.

"Do I look like an axe-murderer?" she asked.

"Well, come at me and I'll see if you're convincing," I replied.

She did.

"Wait a minute… wait a minute… I wouldn't be scared of you. Let me put myself in someone else's shoes."

"Hurry up!" she exclaimed. "We don't have long."

"I know, I know. I'll put myself in Sue's shoes."

I steeled myself and she came at me again.

"Wait… No… Sue wouldn't be scared of you either."

"Oh, come on!"

"Girls," Ben called. And Kay became just another thwarted, would-be axe-murderer.

"Why don't you buy an axe?" Kay asked Ben hopefully.

"You never know when you might need an axe."

"No, we don't need an axe!" he replied.

"Well then, how about a garden hose? You can never tell when one of those will be handy," I asked.

"We don't need one!" Ben was becoming impatient.

"I know, a plastic barrel!"

"Be quiet, girls! I'm working on a plan."

Germany awaited; again we drove.

When at last we approached the border, Ben pulled up short of the customs office. He and Mike began to earnestly discuss in Danish.

Again, Kay and I exchanged looks.

When we retreated from the border, Kay and I began to experience something quite akin to joy. There was definitely something going on here. What had been mere hope until now was being evidenced by this whispering flight. We could barely suppress our squeals, spilling off our tongues words to illustrate this serendipity—"International drug smugglers or spies!"

We stopped at a café, again coffee and broodjes. It was here that they explained to us that we might be putting ourselves at some risk if we were to continue with them. They gave us the option of returning to the highway to seek another ride. They muttered something about smuggling and drugs sewn into the lining of the fur coats.

Now Kay and I became quite overjoyed. "Bonnie and Clyde!" There was no way we were going to back away from this one.

"I told you so!" Mike said to Ben. Ben excused himself and made a phone call.

We all got back into the car. But this time we drove down a little dirt road through a cow pasture. We drove through pastures for a time, finally paralleling a large fence. At last, a break in the fence, then onto a real road and a welcoming sign — Germany.

We spent some days in Hamburg. This time we experienced excellent restaurants, spas, hotels — we shopped until we tired, and Kay and I soon sported lovely, new clothes and fur coats. We were living well, with pretty much every whim satisfied. There were some "business dealings," a few trips to rather questionable locales, but mostly we just enjoyed.

We resumed the journey, taking to the Autobahn. As we sped along, again with drinks and music, Kay and I sang merrily to the Blondie tape; Ben and Mike conversed. We were in a lane moving quite quickly; in the next lane over, the traffic was much slower. Suddenly, a large truck pulled in front of us from the slower lane. We all stared at what was apparently going to be our car smashing into the back of the truck; at the speed we were traveling, this would have been certain doom. In the few seconds left to us, the truck's driver noticed us and pulled over, barely allowing enough space to give ever-composed Mike the chance to maneuver our speeding vehicle deftly between the truck and the median. Our car sped on. Everyone stared for about fifteen more seconds then resumed our activities without comment.

A constant source of annoyance was Ben. Every time a particularly good song was playing and Kay and I were being carried off by it, Ben would suddenly turn the stereo off, turn around to face us, and say:

"Here's the plan…"

"We know the plan! Turn the music back on!"

"There's a new plan."

"We don't care about the plan!"

But we inevitably had to hear "the new plan"—every hour or so.

Here was a case of someone bent on spoiling our perfect moments. Kay and I were having fun and couldn't care less about details, and from the front seat came the incessant sound of Ben coming up with new plans.

In Cologne—new passports; Kay and I became Canadian. A rather tense trip through the dark, thankfully abandoned German-Dutch border, then on to Holland. We stopped shortly for drinks mostly, also food. It was a very small town and a very small inn. I danced with a little person to an old-fashioned juke-box. His only English seemed to be "I love you." He repeated this to me until we left.

Driving, driving, driving, this time through the night. We approached Amsterdam. It was decided that we stop outside the city and put up in a hotel in the small town of Deventer. In the hotel's restaurant, tired of deciding from the foreign fare, Kay and I simply requested, "Bring us something an American would like." They brought us creamed chipped beef on toast. We thought it hospitable of them to make us something to order and as it turned out, we did like it.

Deventer was lovely. We happened to explore an old, working windmill, and we spent some time looking around the town center. But in Amsterdam we had real fun. Life begins there at about eleven o'clock at night. The streets were as packed as before and the revelry was everywhere apparent.

By day there were various meetings with people unknown to us, who sometimes eyed us with suspicion. They spoke with Ben and Mike in Danish usually, but sometimes in German, and so Kay and I would learn pieces of what was really going on, the bigger picture that we had been trying to ignore; we were having such fun, it didn't occur to us that we might suffer dire consequences.

We were forced to very hurriedly vacate our rooms in Deventer. Ben asked if we had our passports and calmly but quickly directed us to the car. The police had been called. All our belongings were left behind. Oh, well, "Bonnie and Clyde!" We had to take back roads into Amsterdam—the highway was apparently too dangerous. It took us a while, but at last we were safely cloaked in city.

We moved to small rooms in an out-of-the-way neighborhood.

One afternoon, as I took a walk, a stranger called to

me from the lobby of another small hotel across from ours—"Hi, Lucy!" Unaware at the time that we were under police surveillance, I took a few steps toward him and realized I had never seen him before. "Hi!" I answered. With a feeling of foreboding, I returned to our hotel.

The next day, Ben and Mike left to pick up "something" in The Hague. They left behind a sizable sum of money and the few new belongings we had so far bought to replace our loss. Most of the money went to new clothes and cosmetics. They were scheduled to return in two days. They never returned.

Kay and I gathered our things, left the hotel, had a quiet lunch, and resumed hitchhiking.

22

HÔPITAL SAINT PIERRE

The sharp patches of oily grass at the side of the highway appeared to me as a lush green, well-kept lawn. Though the brilliant sky seemed cold and dark.

"I've got to rest for a minute," I told Kay. But she couldn't wake me for almost two hours, and the only other life was cars speeding by at sixty miles an hour.

Finally, we reached Brussels. I was in agony—the infection had spread to my blood. I had a fever, was nearly delirious, and it caused excruciating pain to even have the wind blow on me. There was no way I could move my arm. Even the pull of gravity, experienced when getting up and down, was nearly unbearable.

Kay tried her French: "Ou est l'hospital… hospital!" She had forgotten the proper French. Two very similar words—the English hospital and the French hôpital—but pronounced differently enough so as not to be intelligible.

I kept blacking out, wondering how it could be so dark and cold. I felt heightened unreality at the sound of a man playing unfamiliar tunes on an accordion drifting to me from across the street.

It also, we found out, happened to be a national

holiday (something to do with saints). This would not be a problem except that we had no money or a place to exchange some. We were destitute, and I was indeed dying.

The pain I was in began to ebb; I felt comfortable for the first time in weeks. I was warm, and though the day still seemed dark, it was pleasant enough. I tried to convince Kay that we didn't need a hospital anymore. I just needed to sleep.

Kay frenzied herself in her quest, until at last a group of four Moroccan youths came to our aid. They had no car but were willing to help us to the nearest hospital.

It felt like a week's worth of walking; I was mostly being carried. But I remember the gray carnival, the gray flower show, the gray buildings, the gray parks. At last we arrived at the hospital.

The stretcher they put me on was the softest, most comfortable bed I had ever lay down upon. I couldn't figure out why they were wheeling me so quickly—I was getting dizzy. Finally we stopped in some sort of room; I couldn't open my eyes. The nurse tried to raise my arm, excruciating but soon over.

I listened to Kay talk to the doctor about how we hadn't taken drugs; this had been developing for weeks; no, he hadn't taken my blood pressure yet; no, she hadn't realized that I was getting so close to death. "We were just kind of hoping it would go away."

Quite cognizant of the fact that my condition had

prevented showers for many days and that I was really quite filthy, I reassured myself that this doctor was probably some old, unattractive sort. He made me open my eyes.

Here was the most beautiful man I had ever seen or have ever seen since. He looked straight off the canvas of Rossetti. I was now in intense pain and humiliation.

A surgeon came in and, through his workings, caused me to become hysterical with pain; I remember opening my eyes and realizing that he was screaming at me—"Mademoiselle! Mademoiselle!" Then I realized that I also was screaming. We both stopped. I was finally put to sleep.

I was in Saint Pierre for nearly two weeks. I was surprised that they served beer and candy bars for lunch.

And dinner: "What do you want for dinner?" asked my nurse. "The French cheese, the beef tongue, or the escargot?"

"Ha, ha." Obviously he was joking.

"The beef tongue then," he shrugged.

I realized that not only was he serious, but that I was going to get beef tongue for dinner. "The French cheese!" I corrected.

Kay visited twice a day, just enough to torment my nurse, because not only was he "incredibly cute," but he also lent himself to abuse. Or maybe Kay just liked to torment; she threw a rotten peach at him because he told her visiting hours were over.

We found a pen on the floor that had a name taped

on it; we decided it was my nurse's pen. We would, from then on, speak of him as Frank Leeten. For the rest of our days, he would occupy a grand share of our memories and imaginations, yet we never again saw him after I was released from the hospital. He did a novel impersonation of a rabbit.

The first thing I noticed in my post-hospital condition was the large, luxurious coffin store directly across the street. Ambulance chasing, indeed!

Kay had been staying with the Moroccan youths. Now we had nowhere to stay, but instead of looking we bought potato chips called Paprika Chips and sneaked in to a film about the band Kiss. On the way, we saw the Polish Olympic gold medalist pole jumper, or so we thought. I kept forgetting which country we were in. And we were both at a loss as to how to get a city bus to stop, often being taken many blocks from where we wanted to get off.

The Grand Platz—a stunningly beautiful square, intricate and gothic in appearance. We sat in Le Roi d'Espana (one of the sidewalk cafes there), drinking Grand Marnier with a coffee back, and observing, or rather living, the presentation of colored lights and classical music—no doubt a lure for tourists, yet not therefore diminished.

Jean-Paul. I knew him for only a short time, yet he was most deleterious to me.

23

JEAN-PAUL

Kay and I sat outside Saint Pierre one afternoon in the hope of catching a glimpse of either Frank Leeten or the Rossetti doctor of the first night. Oddly, our lack of shelter for the night didn't exercise our worries in the least. We had grown quite accustomed to serendipity.

"I guess we die on the streets tonight."

"Yeah, or maybe someone will chop off all of our limbs!"

We wanted only to be a live-in cook and maid, and we languished over the idea constantly.

Jean-Paul was one of the orderlies at Saint Pierre. He and his friends noticed Kay and me on our bench, eating as usual; soon we were in a lively conversation all together. Curiously, though they were still on duty, they brought us bottles of beer and we planned an evening. Jean-Paul and me, Kay and Michel-Victor.

We descended a stone staircase into a most dungeon-looking room. It was a very lively nightspot. Instead of chairs, there were long benches and tables end to end. We sat down, our feet in puddles of beer; likewise the tables were ashed and spilled upon. The toilets were filthy and had no paper. They played loudly a lot of The Rolling Stones and The Who.

Somehow, Kay and I soon had three or four huge mugs of beer in front of us. We got quite inebriated and still could not finish all that was brought. Jean-Paul dumped the remains on the floor and we left. We piled into a small car; Kay and I, as usual, had no idea where we were going.

I was stunned by Jean-Paul's apartment; we had become quite accustomed to what most Americans would call squalor—this felt like riches. There were two bedrooms and two views; on the bedroom side, Westland Shopping Center, the only American-like mall I had seen in Europe. The other view was of the Flemish community of Anderlecht; one day, while I was taking a walk there, a dog peed on my feet, but it was otherwise splendid. There was a bathtub and a shower in Jean-Paul's apartment and a quite suitable kitchen with several boxes of fast-food paella; terraces ran along both sides of the apartment, connecting all the rooms. The front room was tastefully done—the wallpaper lovely, the furniture luxuriant and comfortable, delightful and detailed tomes of the Flemish masters, a full bar with cigarettes, always stocked (included therein was some fermented egg drink, which we never touched).

Jean-Paul would bring trays of food home from the hospital.

One evening: "What happened to all the dinner trays?"

Kay and I still licking our chops, had to think fast—"Ten men… Ten men came running blindly into the room, overpowered our attempts to subdue them, ran to the refrigerator, grabbed out your dinner trays, gobbled them up, and went running blindly back out again."

Jean-Paul, an obviously gullible blend of obtuseness and paranoia, demanded, "What man? Who are these men?"

"No idea," I answered. "They were gone as soon as they came."

"We're only glad that we escaped with our lives," Kay put in.

Kay and I began to languish; we missed home. Though quite comfortable in foreign climes, we were finally missing our own culture, the geography of our birth.

Jean-Paul was comfortable yet boring. We listened to Bach's organ music. We drank constantly. We read *Jane Eyre* and *The Old Man and the Sea*. We still enjoyed bread with chocolate spread or unsalted butter. We very much appreciated the Museum of Art, especially its Bruegel and Bosch pieces.

Jean-Paul began to betray signs of what would turn out to be a very violent nature. If a man on the street asked me anything or even smiled at me, Jean-Paul would start a fight with him, then later blame me for enticing him. The first time he hit me was because I said his name aloud in a public place. But afterwards he bought me some intoxicating perfume (which I knew to be very expensive), and I was sure his violence would pass.

Kay grew too weary and, for an unnamable reason, depressed. She decided to go home. I couldn't stay without her. This ended our trip.

Jean-Paul accompanied us to London, our desired, economical port of exit. The ship sailed from Ostend to Dover (whose white cliffs looked more like tan to me). The passage was exhilarating; I always liked ships. We sat on deck the entire time (about three hours). On departing the ship, we were asked by an officer to present our tickets. I was entirely unused to understanding a language; I ignored him. He got annoyed and increasingly irritated; he reiterated his request.

"Oh! You're speaking English!" It finally occurred to me. I was likewise surprised to be able to read signs and advertisements — "Oh! It's English!" over and over.

We did some sightseeing — Buckingham Palace, Big Ben, Piccadilly Circus. We stayed the night at the airport; we were flying standby again, so we had to be there earlier than mass transit could deliver us. The very early morning (around 2 a.m.), a bagpipe band came through playing a very enjoyable song. Some Middle Eastern dignitary came in about 5 a.m. and bought tickets for the Concorde.

In the morning, we paid the equivalent of ten dollars apiece for the "American Breakfast," which was two small pancakes and a boiled egg with some weak coffee, and this was in the inexpensive café.

We prepared to board the plane, saying our good-byes to Jean-Paul—a little teary-eyed to be leaving Europe, though not necessarily for leaving Jean-Paul. The security guards at Heathrow were patting down all the passengers and asking various questions. Kay and I bumbled in through the little guide mats, making a scene. "It's this way, you fool!" "Oh, I'm just so sure that you are wrong!" "I'm certain it's this way!" "Your verdict wouldn't hold up in a court of law!" Then, again unused to speakers of English, I loudly over-enunciated: "This is a flute. A flute. It will beep in the metal detector. You know—beep!" I gestured wildly to illustrate my point. We were ushered through with uncharacteristic speed; they didn't pat us down (waving us past when we presented ourselves); they asked no questions. They just wanted us gone.

So we boarded our plane. After a couple of hours in flight, Kay asked, "What's that coastline over there?"

"What coastline? We're over the ocean," I answered.

"No, there's a coastline there," she insisted.

Trying to see what she meant, the only thing I could think of, "You mean that bank of clouds?"

"Oh! I'm not that stupid!" she angrily replied. "You're blind if you can't see it!"

After an hour, her coastline revealed itself to be the wing of the airplane—"Consider the source," I thought.

It was on this flight that I discovered Edward

Gorey; in a moment of exemplary coolness, the airline magazine had an article about him. I quickly came to love his work.

Our quarrelsome nature seemed to entertain the flight attendants. Our last onboard conversation:

"What a smooth landing!"

"I've never experienced so smooth a landing!"

"What a skillful pilot we must have!"

"We must give him our compliments."

A minute later we landed (the usual bumps included).

When we were going through customs, we had the clothes on our backs and a change in a plastic shopping bag, a stuffed geoduck doll, a carton of Gauloises, my flute, and a Stephen King novel.

The agent was confused, perhaps too much to be suspicious:

"How long were you over there?"

"Six months."

She didn't ask the obvious and just let us go our way without comment.

When we left the airport in Seattle (the last leg of our journey to be by car), we only half-comedically kissed our native ground. The next order of business—to eat at a family-style, American restaurant with club sandwiches, weak coffee with free refills, and strawberry-rhubarb pie a la mode—we made a feast of it.

Sue picked us up. She played the tape of a Judy Collins song about dear friends. We were "so glad to see you, my friends."

Sue was accompanied by our grandfather; it was our first meeting (he lived in Tennessee). His letters to me had always been full of life-affirming philosophy; I was so pleased to be meeting him—for about a half of an hour. During this space of time, he proved himself to be the most selfish, whining bastard I had ever met. Further, I had never known anyone to speak as he did—disconcertingly, unbearably slowly: "Well... girls...think I'll... go... up to the... store..."

Sure he had finished his sentence, I asked, "What have you all been doing?"

"...tomorrow," he continued.

He'd had vascular surgery on his legs, was hospitalized briefly for anorexia. (The doctor told my mother that he was the most completely egocentric person he had ever treated.) He was released and went back to Tennessee to live out the remainder of his days, which turned out to be few.

It wasn't a very long time until I started to miss Europe. I missed the architecture, the cathedrals, the art museums, cappuccinos, the bread and butter, Pickwick tea, filet d'Anvers, the interesting coffee houses, and above all, the quick pace and total freedom of the life of a traveler.

Incongruously, I very much sought to be wed. Jean-Paul kept the romance alive by writing and phoning frequently. He planned to come to the States; he did. He was moody and we fought, but I didn't suspect him of the type of deed that I later found him capable of.

So I embraced Jean-Paul and returned to Europe.

The trip back to Brussels was unremarkable; as always, I enjoyed the singular Flemish countryside. We stopped briefly in Bruges to buy some chocolates and a watercolor rendering of a convent there.

Jean-Paul's father met us at the Brussels central train station. He was a large man with no English; we did manage to communicate through the shared language of German. Though I never much spoke to him about it, I was troubled that he had received his higher education at a university in Berlin in the early nineteen forties and that he remembered the experience most fondly.

We were married in a small ceremony at St. Nicholas' Church. The ceremony was in French.

Jean-Paul became immediately morose. He was subject to violent outbursts and psychotic suspicions — he even grew jealous that I wrote to Kay, and he frequently wouldn't allow it.

From then on, I was not allowed to be alone. When Jean-Paul went to work, I had to stay with one of his sisters or his parents. He censored the letters that I sent home and listened to every telephoned word.

The second time he hit me, the cause was that I wouldn't eat a crepe. Not only did he hit me, he locked me in a room for three hours — until his sister came by to visit. He began to hit me without cause at all, and this became a way of life.

I realized I had to convince him to visit the States; it was my only chance. I knew no one here, except his family and friends. I spoke no Flemish, and my French, though out of necessity markedly improved, was not sufficient to aid me in my ultimate goal—I had to leave Jean-Paul.

My grandfather's death was the occasion. Unaware of my aversion to the man, Jean-Paul was duped. I certainly professed a great love of my grandpa; Jean-Paul couldn't very well deny me attending this funeral. We flew home.

I had been embarrassed around my family; I had made such a mess of things. I wondered how to even bring up the subject, but it was so obvious that I was spared having to articulate the verbiage crowding my mind. We shouted over the fact that I read too much, wasted time I could better spend cleaning the house or listening to his flight of ideas. I left the house and began up the street; he chased me down, grabbed my hair and began to drag me back to the house.

"Leave me alone!" I repeated, scared and filled with what I realized with a shock was hatred for this man. No love. No more. At all.

Surprising to me was the number of cars that stopped; I was surprised that any stopped at all.

"Yeah, leave her alone!"

Two men got out of their cars and pulled Jean-Paul away from me. A woman called to me, "Get into the car!"

I thought she thought that Jean-Paul was a stranger.

"He's my husband," I said.

"I don't care, get in the car!"

She drove me to the battered women's shelter. It was very hard to find; one had to go to the police station, find a particular officer, tell your story, only then did one get an address. Men over the age of twelve were not permitted in the house. And we were constantly warned about giving the address out. Many of us were being stalked.

A very troubling trial was going on at the time: A middle-aged woman had been severely beaten by her husband for years, including humiliation—he had once locked her out of the house, completely naked. Then he got himself a girlfriend. He stayed out a lot. He didn't trouble his wife anymore; he took it all out on the girlfriend. So extreme was his abuse of the girlfriend that she had ended up at the women's shelter. Then, with no more girlfriend, he returned enraged to his wife. This time he couldn't beat her enough to satisfy himself, though he had blackened both her eyes, broken her nose, her jaw, and two ribs. She didn't protect herself; she didn't have a very strong will to live anymore. Felt no power in herself. Unsatisfied, he grabbed their sleeping four-year-old son from his bed and began to beat him. A power indeed began to rise in the woman—he had never touched their son before. For a moment she pleaded, but only for a moment.

She took a gun out of a drawer; it took three shots until he lay lifeless. She was only relieved; she cared not at all about jail. This woman was on trial just as I was in the shelter. Justice was served when the charges against her were dropped; she had the right to protect herself and her son.

Jean-Paul was certain that I couldn't divorce him just because of his violent temper. I did. Then I got a menial job to support myself, and I didn't see Europe again for years.

24

UNCOMMON MISCONCEPTION

My new apartment was a semi-furnished studio in a soon-to-be-gentrified area of town. The bed pulled out of the wall like a drawer—I never pushed it in. The kitchen was roomy in comparison with the rest of the studio. Having only a couple of months to settle in, I was nevertheless glad to be joined by newly homeless Sue and Kay. Three in a studio—wall-to-wall mattresses.

We continued with classes at the university, mostly for fun, taking only those classes that sparked our imaginations and paying no attention to degree requirements. We already knew the hidden loophole for higher education, our automatic in—never needing SATs or GEDs, we already had enough credits to enter as juniors. Still, Kay and I refused to let Sue study. "What? Study?" Worse than a stick-in-the-mud, she was a boulder-in-the-quicksand! Kay would snake-dance around Sue and make her play. We were learning for fun and saw no urgency to study, yet we achieved very good GPAs. My favorite classes were Philosophy of Sartre and Camus, Linguistics and, of course, the language classes.

Lying in bed one night, I heard an "Oops!" and giggling from the kitchen; I knew that giggle.

"What did you do?"

"Nothing." Coyly.

I got up and scanned the kitchen. The window was open—no security problems on the ninth floor. I noticed a mound of dirt on the sill and realized that my pet cactus of many years was gone. It didn't survive the fall.

The next eve, on coming home from work, I sought to make some tea. I looked for the large fresh jar of honey—nowhere to be seen.

"Where's the honey?"

Kay giggled again.

"Did you eat it?" I asked, incredulous. Again the familiar giggle. "We don't even have any bread!" She had spooned into herself a large jar of honey. I shouldn't have been too surprised, as I knew her to eat packets of sugar when she was hungry. Eating disorders were unspoken of then.

At school, we found a fellow weirdo: he had bright red hair and wore purple jeans and kept mostly to himself. We chased him down and found him to be a Belgian man named Vik. His only sustenance was vitamin pills—the opposite problem of Kay's and mine.

She was the teacher's assistant in our German class; she mostly taught the colloquial side of things on Fridays, leaving for the professor the grueling task of grammar. For a while we disliked her and sought to torment her. Until one day, she remarked sadly that no one understood her English. Kay and I both instantly melted; we fell hard into love with *Her*. We followed *Her* around the campus; we attended every one of *Her* classes. When we moved to second-year classes, we lost contact with *Her*. And we never found out *Her* name.

While Kay and I were infatuated with *Her*, Sue fell in love with the Russian professor—Andre McGuire. She found he had a listed number and concocted a scheme to see if he was married. I called for her at a time we knew he would be at school:

"Mrs. McGuire?"

"Yes?"

"Mrs. Ethel McGuire?"

"No."

"Oh, sorry, wrong number."

I hung up. "He's married."

Sue moved to San Francisco. Where, GED-less, she achieved a bachelor's in Slavic Languages and Literature from Berkeley. She graduated with honors. She kept in touch, but her life became entirely separate from mine.

25

IM ABENDSOHNENSHEIN

I opened a small drawer in my desk and pulled from a large wad a fifty-dollar bill. Kay and I were treating our church-mice boyfriends to pizzas topped with lamb and sun-dried tomatoes. The dinner was good and we ordered well drinks for hours — Scotch/rocks mostly.

We quit the restaurant to roam the city. I liked to blow; I would wear billowy clothes and stand on a curb and just blow in the wind. It was all I could think of to do. I was sorrowful often under the weight of Life (as worthy of a capital as God).

As we strolled along the park on the river's edge, church-mouse Sam recounted his jumping from a fifth-story window in an attempt to end his life. (We never used the word "suicide" when speaking of such events or desires — it seemed either too dramatic or too clinical.) The falling he experienced as almost religiously freeing, as intense as flying; but hitting the ground was a completely jarring, bone-splintering event. His legs took five months to heal. His attempt had just seemed like the thing to do at the time; he never tried again.

I thought often of jumping. I would beg friends to join me; they would "play along" for a minute, then laugh at me — though thinking they were laughing with me. I wasn't laughing. I just didn't want to bear the extreme loneliness of such an act, of both trying and achieving. However, I desperately wanted to fall, free, hand in hand with a good friend. It seemed a blessed way to complete a life.

So we walked and blew.

The next evening we rode the terrifying carnival rides where death was imminent. Swearing to God — if he would just let us live — we would never ride one again. Then as we exited safely, we excitedly planned another go at it — again begging God for survival.

The church-mice decided to pool their funds and go get another drink; Kay and I had other plans.

We bought LSD from a street vendor. After twenty minutes, I could feel the unique acid high begin. It would probably take about ten hours and then a deep, restoring sleep to cure me of my distorted thinking.

I had no idea whether I had to go to the bathroom or not or if I had already peed my pants. I decided to take precautionary measures. Serendipitously, a bathroom materialized in the park. The walls and floor inside were bright red, causing me to wonder if I was actually a tampon. The toilet bewildered me; I couldn't figure out how to flush it. Likewise the sink presented an enigma. Oh, well. "Perhaps I'm water," I thought. I couldn't feel myself as solid. And I could feel the weight of myself so I knew I was not air. Furthermore, I couldn't feel any difference between myself and the water in the sink. Once outside, I thought I might jump into and osmose with the river, but a warning feeling kept me from flying into the water's cold depths.

I peeled a piece of trodden-upon candy corn off the sidewalk; Kay and I each ate half. We found a set of dentures, which Kay kept and used for years as an ashtray. It always amazed me the things that occurred when one was on acid. Incredible things, bizarre things, things that wouldn't happen if you were sober. Things not the result of the chemicals in one's mind, but things that really happened, as if God provided humor for himself by, in the spirit of Loki, perplexing and confounding one. One time in a canyon, a plane flew overhead; simultaneously, all our hair stood on end and floated around in the sun.

We spent hours in a grocery store, perusing the intricacies and colors of the items, making sure to steer clear of the horrifying produce section. I wanted a bread item but somehow got lost in the salad dressing aisle; I wandered into pet food, despairing that I would never have my bread; finally, I came across a poppy seed bagel lying on a box of corn flakes. Another God-trick probably, but I was most grateful. In a J obsession, we bought Jube Jels, Jolly Joes, and juice to give out on the street, most people turned us down, but one man said, "Sure I'll have a Jube Jel"—this we found most pleasurable. I was "Jennifer" in my lace skirt and Kay was "Joe" in her black, zippered jacket. And we returned to the river to walk and sit on the docks.

I kept experiencing earthquakes, though no one else seemed to feel them. I was hyper-alert in anticipation of nuclear warfare and was startled by every sound. Perhaps most disturbingly, I assumed the persona of a late night talk show host; I became Tom Snyder, lost all my own identity. I couldn't escape this inundation of my being, finally I just let it be.

At home I enjoyed the kaleidoscopic movements in my paintings and the little doll that kept beckoning me to come to her in a New York accent. Potato men stood in my dining room having a social gathering. People came out of the walls, walked a minute, gestured, then faded into thin air.

It was only after hours of creative taxation that I finally fell into a comaesque sleep, which I knew would be followed by the acid hangover — something akin to the weakness of terminal illness.

26

A VISIT TO THE BOOKSTORE

Kay and I sprawled over the bus bench; too much Stoli had been imbibed. Kay used my favorite lace handkerchief to wipe the vomit from her face and clothes. Curiously (maybe we looked better than we felt), an old Toyota pulled up to the curb. Who knows why we went with him — adventure?

"Do you like bookstores?" Dick asked.

"Oh, of course!" Thinking of Powell's and the like.

He stopped at Sinful Cindy's Adult Books. I wasn't drunk enough not to be embarrassed. I stared at the floor to avoid all the toys hanging on the walls, the posters, books and films. Kay, on the other hand, laughed and picked up various items and thumbed through magazines with a complete lack of inhibition. Dick steered us to some booths in the back. We squeezed into the one-man booth, first Kay, then me, then Dick. On the rather small screen flashed lively acts of the rather bizarre sort — sadomasochism, including mutilation and sex that required a full bladder.

I felt Dick's hands wander over my breasts and grope between my legs — unacceptable. I tried to fend him off while not looking too hard at the screen. Kay (more drunk than I) agreed to switch places with me, she didn't mind being next to Dick. She laughed in delight at the screen; her tampon alone prevented penetration.

Perhaps realizing this venue wouldn't work, Dick announced that he had to check on something at work. We rode with him down to the dock.

He left the car, walked the short distance to an office and went inside. Kay and I waited for what seemed a lengthy enough span of time. Then we left to see what kind of ship was docked there, with serendipity it would be Russian—alas, it was Filipino. We boarded nevertheless. The rest of the night was lucrative, though not memorable.

In the morning, we went for coffee and eggs at The Copper Kitchen. Kay then realized she had, in her drunken state, given Dick her correct work address—a popular nightclub in the city's center. Indeed, a couple of nights later he showed up. Her co-workers smirked at her apparent choice of partners. (Perhaps they never did things purely to irritate themselves.) She ignored him until he went away.

The bartender at her workplace fell in love with her. "Oh, boy! Free drinks!" I thought. Anyway, I liked him. There ensued a brief relationship; she found him annoying yet amusing. One day, as they were walking from the grocery store in the animation of a light-hearted conversation, he walked head first into a lamppost—peals of laughter from her, a red face from him. I was witness to their only love-act. I was in the same room—she didn't care if I was there or even if he was; she blew gum bubbles into his face and tapped her fingers on his back. I don't know how he felt about the sleeping arrangements, but he was passionate in the act, ignoring her insouciance.

He kept a drawing of Edward Gorey's *The Doubtful Guest* she had done hanging on his wall for years. Kay and I were indeed Doubtful, and The Guest was our mascot. She saw this bartender only a handful of times; she fell in love with someone else. We were always in love with "someone else"—for me it was never reciprocal. Love seemed only a linear equation; I longed for the cyclic.

Kay left for a term to go to Europe with her "someone"—Mike. In a mainly Kay-ish fashion, she managed to get quite ill due to the ingestion of an apparently tainted dried apricot from a filthy sidewalk in Barcelona. But it was still a beloved town, owing largely to the spectacular architecture of Antonio Gaudí—whose works in appearance are very similar to a Dr. Seuss creation.

The conceptions of ancient, dank stones made into manifest reality exacerbated Mike's asthma. They went to a few museums; she showed him the Eiffel Tower; they had the Venetian pizza diavola. They came home—to my delight.

For a time things continued like before. I had some episodes—like lying nude on the bathroom floor, unable or unwilling to communicate. But mostly I was okay, I was still able to work and take care of myself.

Still, the beginnings of illness by increments removing me, first from adventure, then from life, caused Kay to feel abandoned. We had shared everything—what to study at school, what books to read. We preferred the same restaurants, the same films, the same interior design. But I was soon to retreat from the world into vaguery, and she would be left to fend for herself. She never forgave me.

27

JUMP-OFF JOE CREEK

"You're so much fun to be with." Curious as it was, he provided all the transportation and funding. It's easy to come up with ideas when someone else facilitates. And Steve indulged my every whim and fancy.

One evening, we sat in a comfortable restaurant finishing something—fish? Anyway, I saw a brochure about Nevada; it mentioned something about Winnemucca. Another bit of whimsy:

"Let's go!" I wanted.

"Well, okay. We'll leave tomorrow." His reply.

"No, now!" I wondered at the best way to accomplish my end.

"All right," him trying to calm me. "We'll pack a bag and be on the road."

"But no! We have to go right now! We'll just pay this bill and go!" So we left.

The clear night's moon beautified the passing hills and woods and occasional farm. It was on this trip that I learned of the existence of Jump-Off Joe Creek. And took my first tour of Ashland; the streets there all had Shakespearean names. Though it was late and this a small town, the streets bustled with activity. It was a wonderful town. The population was surely very literary, with visitors aplenty to the Shakespearean stages famed there.

We stopped for coffee in Yreka, at some family-owned version of Denny's. It was getting quite late. We drove on, listening to Vangelis on the stereo.

On finding myself in California, I made a change of plans.

"I want to go to San Francisco." My sister lived there with her husband Jim and my one-year-old niece Lily (I was forever to call her Smin), whom I had yet to meet.

Steve changed destinations, as if the new plan better suited him as well; he had a brother there.

Nearing Lake Shasta (with its horrifying bridge), our headlights went out. The night was black, no lights anywhere and no phone for who knows how far? We inched forward, relying on the blinker lights to see for us. One second we could barely see, the next we saw nothing.

At last, an exit with some kind of life, a little gas station. The mechanic wouldn't be in until morning (three hours later). We bought corn chips and coffee in the mini-mart. Another traveler pulled in. As it happened, he had a bit of mechanical training; he and Steve fixed the car. Steve tried to give him twenty bucks but he turned it down. Back en route to SF!

We knocked on my unsuspecting sister's door. She and husband Jim were delighted (thank God). The moment I saw Smin, I loved her completely. She could have as easily been my own. I loved her unconditionally and I always would.

We ate fruit salad in Golden Gate Park. We went to a Russian bookstore. We walked along the "decaf skinny latte" drinkers' streets. We visited the marina taken over by wild sea lions. I bought Nabokov's *Pale Fire* at City Lights Bookstore (this turned out not to be one of my favorites of his).

I phoned my other tie to San Fran—Dasha. It had been years since I last saw her. We walked. She said it was her policy not to let newcomers to the city ride on public transportation, so one could get a real sense of the city. We did get quite a fill of the town. We walked past clothing designers' shops. We went to Chinatown. We sat in a bar and had a few. We caught up on each other's lives. And the body politic.

Due to conflict of schedules, Steve had to go back after one night. I stayed, having enough for a train.

"Those are tourist things!" Sue protested about Jim's plans for me.

"She is a tourist!" Jim countered.

I was happy to see the tourist sights. The most crooked street in the world. Fisherman's Wharf (an abundance of candy shops and bakeries). And of course, a ride on the trolleys, where the conductor let me ring the bell.

The train ride home was most aesthetically pleasing. The ocean, forests, streams… Sue had baked for me a dozen bran muffins; they were quite good. The trip took a while, but I loved to travel.

Steve met me at the train station. That night we supped at the docks; appealing in that no one was ever around, yet great acts of labor were performed continuously. It seemed like the factory machinery was the only thing left in a world that had once been populated by selves made of flesh and bone.

I never suspect anyone of racism. It is something I just presuppose no thinking being would ever agree with. So my shock was complete when Steve compared a blood transfusion between a black person and a white person with a white person and a monkey. Shock indeed! Then outrage. He could never redeem himself of this. I made him leave my apartment right away. I told him I would never see him again. I never did.

28

INFINITY FACTORIALIZED

Dell's was, for the time, the finest restaurant in the city. I would make salad dressing, mayonnaise, and pâté. The house bakers sent up loaf upon loaf of baguettes, and for Sunday brunches they would send trays of fresh baked croissants and muffins.

My forte was appetizers; I especially liked making fruit and cheese plates; for fruit they had blood oranges, kiwis, mangoes, and guavas; for cheese they had Brie, Jarlsberg, Muenster. It was decided one day that the dishes weren't uniform; there were apparently complaints. We were going to have to do all the dishes in uniform. "Great!" I thought, "I'm going to have to learn a new way to do everything."

"I want them done the way Lucy does them."

Not only did I not have to change my ways, but I was getting also compliments.

Easter brunch. Decidedly the busiest shift of the year. I was fatigued beyond anything I had ever experienced, and slowly I made my way to the break room.

"How much are we paying you, Lucy?" my boss asked.

"Seven dollars an hour."

"Make it eight." And he was as good as his word; my raise was even retroactive starting with that shift.

At night, the waiters would take pieces of baguette and play basketball with the busboys, aiming for empty bus tubs across the room. They talked about the mighty aloe plant, once tall and proud, now an amputee. There were only stubs where we had clipped, in order to obtain the curative gel within; this was dubbed "the sad demise of the Great Aloe." The dishwashers were all communists; they posted party information and they sold newsletters. They were very hard workers; they sought out chores if ever there was a lull time. The turnover (in restaurants usually quite high) was almost nonexistent. They spread their ideology to anyone interested.

Every night we made Chicken Moutarde to feed the employees. The boss always sent beer to the kitchen, or on especially busy nights he sent champagne.

I met a woman one night, a new baker in the restaurant. Her name was Dianne. We walked home together. We decided to get a drink. An Italian bar was reeling in activity. We had to talk loudly to be heard. We ordered Champagne, then Scotch/rocks and finished off with Grand Marnier with coffee back.

Dianne thought it impossible the way so many people sat stone-faced while listening to the symphony. As she watched and heard, tears streamed down her face and she sat rapt in profound Pain or, at other times, Joy. We both thought it hubris to say things such as "Classical music is relaxing." Pachelbel's "Canon", for instance, someone said was mellow. To me that piece is poignant, depressed but without despair; in fact, the pain in it is almost sweet, but there is most certainly intense pain in it. Classical music is very emotional, there is Rage, Rapture, Passion; it can be frenzied one moment and reflexive the next. There is sheer genius there.

Dianne and I took a taxi to her apartment; it had hardwood floors with a Persian rug spread upon. The chairs appeared to have been crafted by Picasso. We spread out on mattresses in a glassed-in porch; it made kind of a fort, a nest. There were lots of pillows and lots of blankets. We undressed each other slowly; we kissed each other deeply. I felt for parts of her body that I knew from mine were made the source of ecstasy, more than pleasure, when touched. We lay all night thus: my hands on her; her hands on me.

My heart felt a spark; it flared for a moment that night, but it burned itself out in swift order.

I quit working at the restaurant, opting to go to school, another attempt, this time for a more lucrative nursing degree. I didn't think again of Dianne for years.

29

MICHAEL LOVED BOOKS

I loved books and Michael. I never knew if Michael loved me. I loved him so much that I didn't care if he chose me, as long as he had someone to love and to love him. It was very important to me that someone love him as much as I did.

I would have let him beat me, insult me, even urinate on me. I couldn't think of anything that he might do that would diminish my love for him. I don't think he cared.

We worked together in a small diner. He was a waiter, I a cook. We lived in the same building. He was on the sixth floor, I in the basement. He could call to me from the window of his apartment and we could arrange to meet, to go out, whatever...

While walking home from work, he would throw quarters, handfuls of them, so that someone might happily stumble upon them and think it serendipity. We always stopped at McDonald's for a fifty-cent vanilla cone.

Sometimes we'd go to a little bar called The Hobbit Hole. We always ordered beer; I hated beer. We wouldn't get inebriated, just alleviated. I don't think he ever noticed how I noticed him. What shirt? What tie? Which shoes? Clean-shaven? On and on, I so loved to drink in his details.

He was a seasoned shoplifter. He walked out of a discount store with a new, unpaid for, vacuum cleaner. He adorned his apartment with wealth accumulated from theft. When creditors called, he would concoct absurd stories:

"Oh, he no longer lives here. He went to a psychiatric hospital in upstate New York; it turns out he has manic-depression—he tried to kill himself."

For some reason, the creditors must have believed him; he never heard from one twice.

A favorite pastime was to go look at vacant apartments together. He said he liked to know the market for rentals; I liked pretending that we were married. It was fun to see them and imagine my belongings and self in them.

He had a cat—Barney. I loved "Biff." He was the most expressive cat I've ever encountered. He looked terrified, sleepy, nervous… insane. We would play games with his personality traits: "He's the baddest." "The cruelest." "The meanest." "The sadisticest." "The slyest." "The craftiest." "The worst." "The least sincere." "The connivingest." We always said we were going to "tie him up, skin him out, and fry him up for dinner." Somehow the thought of him as dinner endeared him to me.

Michael and I played a game similar to Dungeons

and Dragons, though considerably less detailed. I continually lost because every time I had money and opportunity, I bought a beast. I loved to buy beasts. They were in the game solely as a means to carry the necessary gold. But I couldn't be bothered with gold—just beasts.

Michael was attracted to men as well as women. Once we ingested some MDA; we planned a fun evening. I ended up having to wait in my apartment for hours while he turned a trick—more about lust for sex than lust for money. But I enjoyed listening to Russian folk songs. And later we did walk through a forested park to sneak into the zoo.

The only sexual experience 'twixt Michael and me happened in an outdoor amphitheater; it just turned out to be in the middle of the day and a rather popular venue for lunchers. We had an audience, but were left alone by police. The only body parts exposed were the ones essential for the missionary position. It was a memory. But it didn't do justice to my love. I mainly fantasized about sleeping in his arms, spending all my nights there. Sex—so what?

Just that once turned out to be safe for me.

But I watched Michael die of AIDS.

30

A POET

Rick was a poet. His view of the world was of a beautiful poem. His everyday language was as if he were quoting something enchanting. He called me his muse.

He likened my poetry to Sylvia Plath's; I had been afraid he would find it ordinary, facile or pretentious. But he saw beauty there. He kept after me to submit. After wholeheartedly rejecting that notion for months, I was finally worn down; I submitted a short story. This first attempt bore fruit, giving me momentum to try for future accomplishment.

Rick had a studio apartment in an old Victorian-style house. An entire wall was filled ceiling to floor with books. I hadn't known anyone to have more books than me. He treated me to many titles I had overlooked: a Nabokov book, *Bend Sinister*, and a novel by Leonard Cohen, *The Favorite Game*.

He was the only man I've ever known who loved the world as much as I did. We loved to sing and adored the act of play; we raced each other down Waterfront Park and did silly dances on the beach or in empty streets. He was as bewildered as I was by the alphabet and found addition almost beyond reckoning, at the same time admiring the beauty of the Grand Unified Theory, and, of course, we were inseparable from literature.

He smoked cigarettes incessantly, more than even me (and I was a die-hard smoker). He couldn't even sit through a movie without at least one smoke break. Coupled with advancing years, the endless cigarettes caused what was diagnosed as congestive heart failure. He wheezed and his breath rattled in his chest, and always when he tried to laugh, he choked. I didn't encourage him to stop smoking as the doctors did. It was too late, and for a few extra months of life he would be in the great discomfort of withdrawal.

We crossed an ocean beach. The loose sand in the wind blew over the solid ground in a kaleidoscope of design. He told me that he loved me. I loved him too, but I couldn't face it at the time. So I said nothing—maybe just an "Oh" with a nervous laugh.

Nearly a year after his unrequited confession, he died.

31

BROTHERHOOD AND FREEDOM

Craig was my friend. We were communists together. We passed many engrossing hours discussing politics and philosophy and the absurdity of things like ears—on into night after night, draining endless pots of herbal tea. Days filled with nude beaches seen through the eyes of MDMA highs, analyzing the color orange and wondering at the popularity of plain potato chips. We dutifully participated in many protests where we were told by red-blooded Americans to go back to Russia, only to be told later in our own homes by fellow "comrades" that our libraries didn't contain enough radical books.

The first time I met Craig, I was sitting at the bar in a café where I worked, examining aloud with great dismay the multiple misspellings on the menu and writing out "Better Dead Than Red" with my lipstick on the mirrored countertop. We fell into a discussion about Grenada, a socialist island paradise at that time, and discovered that we both longed to live there. We planned an evening tryst.

The first thing that I noticed about Craig's apartment was his staggering collection of books. I perused at length the beckoning titles—so much Russian literature! A soulmate! Works of Nabokov, Bulgakov, Turgenev, almost everything written by Dostoevsky! Also the huge tome of the life of Emma Goldman—the most inspiring life story ever penned! Nearly every author was one I also enjoyed; so many of the titles were ones I had also read. We started a lasting conversation that night. And for the first time, perhaps the only time in my life, I knew physical love that bonded heart and mind and didn't take into account a separate self.

We both celebrated the individual and disdained the frequent Marxist appellation "the masses." Though I was spiritual and he an atheist, we agreed that religion isn't so much "the opium of the masses" as their LSD or something such. He had grown up in such a hilariously conservative, Christian environment that he could regale me at length with impossible anecdotes of his youth. While attending a prayer meeting at the age of ten, he had been sick all over a living room chair. He had been feeling ill all day as a result of eating something disagreeable, and the queasiness had finally caught up with him. Instead of being upset about the furniture or concerned about his health, the minister was delighted—"It's the devil coming out of him!" And everyone sang out praises for Jesus.

He would accompany me though on my trips to the Unitarian church. He enjoyed the sermons (they were decidedly more philosophical than religious) and loved the music. Once an intern minister gave a sermon concerning impoverished people that cared not about all the good intentions of the affluent: "When it comes down to it, they'll say 'I was hungry and you didn't feed me.'" She pulled no punches. This sermon disturbed the patrons of the church, as they were very much satisfied that their good intentions were enough. For the first time that Craig and I had seen, people began to get up and leave rather than meet the challenge of this sermon. Craig was so very impressed that at the end of the service he could only babble in what he claimed was incoherence at the minister. He felt foolish, yet he made a large donation.

The Party friends we had were bothered that we went to any church. They also objected to my face makeup and the fact that I dressed in anything other than torn blue jeans. I was a lipstick communist. These friends perplexed me further in that when we had picnics or other community dinners, they had to purposely burn the food and make sure that the bread was stale, etc.... Somehow, they equated not suffering with causing suffering. Craig and I gradually extricated ourselves from the Party. We had our own unique belief system and no one was doing it right. We dreamed of anarchism, with perhaps communism or a benign dictatorship in the interim years.

Craig and I moved into an apartment together. It had shining hardwood floors, a glassed-in porch, and a deep claw-footed bathtub. It was situated one block from a wonderful reparatory cinema, whose reparatory was the bizarre and unusual. It was there that I first saw *Eraserhead* (we both developed a lasting appreciation for David Lynch) which was double-billed with the much older, though no less intriguing, *Freaks*. *Walkabout* was also featured, the soundtrack of which gave me my first appreciation of Stockhausen. One block in the other direction took you to a dimly lit coffee house crowded with books and journals — the first I knew to offer a variety of freshly ground beans, and where smoke was thick in the air. Close by was a cheap Chinese restaurant, an excellent venue for extremely cheap well drinks. The neighborhood grocery store sold an interesting array of produce — lychee nuts and loquats and many varieties of oranges. It was the least expensive area in the city; we paid $140 per month for our one-bedroom home.

Besides the eclectic multitudes of students and old folk, artists and musicians also thrived in the area. One could wear pajamas to the store for coffee in the morning; no one paid attention to details like what clothes were worn. Everyone was assimilated into a community that took on an almost familial air.

It was the first time that I'd so enjoyed living with someone. I found, to my surprise, that I didn't resent lack of privacy. I didn't mind if he shaved while I bathed, nor if he talked on the phone as I watched *Land Sharks* on the television. It was soothing to read as he read, each lost in our own printed worlds but ever aware that we were together. We took turns choosing music—sometimes Bach, sometimes The Partridge Family or Iggy Pop. We used to lie on the floor and writhe to Brahms' *Fourth Symphony*.

We took wine glasses to a rusty boat dock in the rain and dangled bare feet in the Willamette, waiting for barges to pass by and jolt us with waves. On the way home we dug deep and gave all our money to a man trying to cover himself with cardboard in a patch of sopping, muddy weeds.

The next night we spent on a ledge behind a fountain's waterfall, doing our best to sing Borodin's *Polovtsian Dances* and make up stories to entertain each other:

"One day Mundo Fundo Ichabod Shay O'Day approached you in the city's heat to request something long forbidden—iced tea…"

We took a short trip to the beach. We sped past mountains of oyster shells—I wondered how the creatures mated. We took a long walk down a pebbly beach and collected what we were sure were priceless gems. The salty clean air was dizzying. I wrapped myself in long ribbons of seaweed. Together we danced to the music of the ocean—a song peppered by the screeching of gulls. Once again, I enjoyed standing on that last bit of land, knowing how much was there—facing the water we embraced its vastness and power; facing the other direction we embraced a continent.

We pleased ourselves for hours by admiring words that we considered beautiful—"tempestuous…

sepulchered... languishing..." And sometimes more frivolous amusement, finding words that formed other words when pronounced backwards—news/swoon, road/door, thread/dearth...

We gave our hearts to a stray cat—a male tabby yclept Bubastis. "Bast" would tear around the room at such a pace that he would actually gain enough momentum to run on the walls. He loved taking baths with us and was quite fond of bagels.

We explored interesting theories of our own conceiving. Craig thought that perhaps everyone in the world had an individual experience of colors, seeing what we could allname but perhaps in one's eyes was completely different from others'. Each seeing colors that the other couldn't imagine, as one can't imagine an entirely new color.

Having always born a deep desire to bear a child, I was in bliss at discovering I was with one. Craig and I spent long whiles contemplating names, and our bookstore attention turned solely to those volumes essential to a child's library—*Scalawagons of Oz*, *Too Many Daves*, *Estherhazy*... We read aloud to the developing child the poetry of Lewis Carroll, including "Jabberwocky" in both English and German, and excerpts from *The Master and Margarita*. We played music and danced, knowing our child was experiencing, for the first time, the joy of music and movement.

At six months two weeks pregnant, our little girl died.

I had never contemplated so profound a loss. I never shed a tear. I was speechless. For days I avoided Craig's eyes as if they would destroy me, but I finally found my only solace there; we alone truly knew what had occurred. My anguish became complete when I learned that I would never be able to bear a child. I sought no other company. I wanted reality to end. I remember being glad that it ceaselessly rained, perhaps God also felt our loss. I don't think that I could have borne the sun. I couldn't return to work.

We went to Flanders. The small town of Bruges we found to be the most splendid, almost religiously beautiful, example of the best works of man and God. We spent hours in the stunning grand cathedrals and churches, the walls of which were covered with the dark and reverent works of Rubens and Van Dyck. We lunched on bread and cheese on the banks of canals where myriad swans floated and over which ancient stone footbridges crossed. The fields and gardens were crowded with Wordsworth's "hosts of golden daffodils." The narrow streets were filled with little shops, in front of which sat old women making by hand exquisite pieces of lace. All around were little bakeries and confectioneries bursting with intricately formed marzipan and chocolates and huge speculaas fresh from their carved wooden molds. All this beauty contrasting with our daughter's death, we took turns reading to each other from the works of John Milton:

> *Hail divinest Melancholy,*
> *whose saintly visage is too bright*
> *to hit the sense of human sight;*
> *And therefore to our weaker view*
> *O'erlaid with black, staid Wisdom's hue.*

But the grandeur of Flanders could be almost ecstatic, as Jacques Brel surely knew:

> *Aye, Marieke! Marieke!*
> *Come back again!*
> *Come back again to Brugges and Gand!…*
> *Mein platte land! Mein Flanderland!*

Curative Flanders gave us strength to return home.

I was forced to look for new employ, as the little café where I had been working had gone out of business — one of the implicating factors being the kicking, by one of the owners, of the state inspections person in the behind as he bent to pick up a dropped pen. The owners then sold the café and moved to Amsterdam. As it turned out, I would never hold another job.

32

SCHIZOPHRENIA

I've never been glad that I didn't kill myself when I had the strength. I remember hearing a song; the message: think about the future, life won't always be bad. But that's not true; life can be one continuous drowning in a lake of fire.

Coming back from Europe, I was sad to leave adventure behind, but I also missed home. I thought at the time there would be plenty of time to enjoy further adventure. What I didn't know was that my Life would shortly end.

What was later named the beginning of illness was intensely enjoyable to me. My only problem was that my thoughts were beginning to ache. But I was held in complete awe over the world, suddenly magnificent. I was seeing colorful light flashes everywhere. Colors and textures were more beautiful than structures, and structures overcame the sky.

Going for cigarettes, I found the beauty osmotic; the rain, the low, flat sky, the streets advancing like wet sticks of gum into infinity. This was euphoric; people would wonder what drug I was on (not a new experience, though). I stared at the lights dancing on the wall in my bedroom, the bathroom mirror held me spellbound, and my globe provided hours of fascination. I listened to The Irish Rovers or "The Wall." Under the spell of much grandeur, I climbed a fence into someone's backyard with the sole purpose of embracing a tree there. It was unfurling its resurrected life too early— there was still the chance of ice. I prayed for that tree, for its courage in being the first to bring green back to a pencil-drawn world. So, on that sodden, late winter day, I kissed the tree with easy tears for the fragility and extreme beauty surrounding everything.

So it was that I one day found myself welling up with joy as I passed a tree turning pink; I was tearing up with happiness when I heard a voice, more clear than the passing cars, it said: "You could die in a field of flowers."

From that moment, a veil was drawn; everything was gray and threatening. I passed through a period of complete non-feeling. My love for Craig was not diminished, but I could no longer feel it. I was slowly sinking down a hole. It was soon that my daily existence meant, at the most, a benign, constant edginess, but often it meant howling panic. From that single voice came many; they were my constant tormentors. They marked me in illness. An illness that to me meant a world thoroughly impossible to negotiate. I couldn't easily cross streets, as I had no idea if there were cars speeding down on me or if they were parked along the sides. I was horrified at finding my hands dipping razors deep into my arms. This was something I knew wasn't me. The easier explanation from my voices: my movements were all being controlled by a computer; this computer was programmed by people who understood God and carried out his will. I could feel myself being made to act, whether to sign my name, or lift a glass, or put a cigarette out on my arm. No movement of mine came from my own free will. I no longer remember how many years passed until I no longer saw Craig; the last thing I remember about him was his distressed look and cries, as I was being dragged off to a seclusion room.

An angel of God appeared to me three times; each time he said that I was the reincarnation of the chief of the secret police under Stalin, Lavrenti Pavlovich Beria, a man who had tortured and maimed multitudes in the name of state security. So, the angel informed me that I must hurt myself—that I would be controlled to hurt myself until my misery became complete, and redemption would be at hand only after I pushed metal forks into my eyes for the world's recompense. My life became fully mired in fear.

At first, I was able to mask the torment within. I learned to be able to read faces for the correct response, though booming voices kept me from hearing anything else. I used books as props, so that it seemed I was laughing or crying at the contents therein and not the truth—voices. I was able to disguise my extreme agitation by sheer dint of good acting skills—I always pretended I was playing a part. At first my heightened anxiety compelled me to try anything; I briefly put hope in medication.

At first I thought the side effects were new symptoms of my psychosis. I was suicidal at the thought that it was the illness that deprived me of all thought—I literally never had a thought in my head, I could only respond: "Oh." "Yeah." "Okay." I couldn't go outside without an extreme allergic reaction to the sun, which caused me to break out in burning, itching welts. My jaw held itself painfully askew, veering off to one side, and I couldn't relax it. My hands shook so badly that I couldn't sign my name.

At last I stopped taking the pills. At first it was wonderful. Thoughts flooded my head. I entertained myself for hours with just thinking. I had unbounded energy. I didn't sleep at all for two and a half weeks. But shortly voices deluged me again; fear came back as well. I began seeing little demons hiding themselves in corners and scurrying about.

Enough symptoms finally surfaced to land me in the hospital; this began a continual battle with chemical lobotomies. I still tried with all my strength to resist my mind and make it perform the tasks it knew so well: eating, showering, reading. I kept trying to finish school in between hospitalizations. Yet so chemically infused was I that I had a grand mal seizure in the microbiology lab. I tried to reason my way to health without the use of chemicals. My school days ran down. I couldn't fight this illness with a frightening name; they pronounced it Schizophrenia, to me it meant death. I juggled classes, blaming them for my inability to function. Eventually, I just locked myself in the bathroom for hours and let my life go. The stereo talked, or rather, communicated with me. It soothed me to the reality of death. No control was my own. Music ushered in the alter-worlds. Dark... Dark... Push razors deep into my breasts, and lit cigarettes. No more reality. Or rather intense, profound reality. A pseudo world abandoned in music, crescendo of feeling. A release from the obligation of knowing, washing over me like waves of balm; spiraling into my own unfamiliar mind, an intimate relationship.

Maim, maim... No pain, no pain. Lost in sensate found. Manifest controllers — "Give in... Don't fight..." words coming from the music, words hidden from the music's words. More manifest than my real body. Like a dark, abjectly strange circus. In a separate world the stereo speaks only to me. Down, down, language of the mind — surreal yet concrete, velvet... soft... doors.

Threatening, nervous and agitated, the only course is mutilation. Powerful, screaming melodies, unable to ignore — the only reality force, life force, controlling force, frightening force.

The state hospital was ancient; the windows were barred. It looked ominous yet beautiful in its way, and the grounds were extensive and impressive.

This beautiful façade belied the truth within. I would end up spending years of my life there.

I never got used to the seclusion room — a cold, dark blue, bare, cement and windowless cell, where I often endured the further agony of leather restraints. All I wanted was to move, and they made it so I couldn't. Time was grossly distorted; there was no way to measure it. The light bulb in the ceiling perpetually gave off its low watt, yellow illumination. I was left with only the tormenting, faceless voices for company; I had an intense yearning for a physical presence to share with this existence. I needed to know there was someone else on Earth; I needed to know how many hours... days...

The ward was crowded; people shrieked and cried. They begged for cigarettes and sent trays of food flying. For some reason, it was quite common for patients to roam the ward naked. There was no calm, just moments more or less dramatic.

I was overwhelmed and trying to hide from the world, trying to hide from God. I curled up in a plastic lime-green chair.

"Why don't you go to your room to sleep?" one of the attendants asked.

"I can't find it," I answered.

He said he'd show me. He took my hand and led me to a room—an empty room.

He opened the door. I noticed only the bed and was glad to curl up on it. But he followed me onto the bed. I tried to keep my clothes on. I couldn't scream—I could barely whisper. I resisted; I told him I liked my clothes on. "She doesn't want to! She doesn't want to!" I repeated about myself. He grabbed a handful of my hair and forced my head down. He threatened to hit me. He was large and strong. He hurt me. As he finished, he said that if I told anyone they would never believe me because I was crazy and that they would surely give me shock treatment (this he knew was an obsessive fear of mine, which I had been threatened with before). I put my clothes back on, and though I was warm, further wrapped myself in two blankets—convinced that I now had AIDS. After several hours, I was discovered in the room where the attendant had left me. I wanted to cry but I was too scared. The nurse who found me decided I had broken the rules; I spent the next eight hours in seclusion as a penance.

I didn't know how to keep safe. My voices only instructed me to put my head through a window. At a loss—I did. A gash on my scalp bled profusely. I got stitches and transferred to another ward. I wondered how much longer I would live.

For many months I did not breathe the outside air. I watched the sun rise and fall through a window. I watched the seasons change.

Christmas more than all else was torturous. With all the symbolism and music — the beauty, memories, hope — "Born that man no more may die." Then why does He let me die? I was far from home in a dark, cold place. Some attempt was made to deck the ward, but this only made me lonelier. My Christmas present that year was a pack of generic cigarettes. On the day itself, I was strapped to a chair for six hours because I had cut myself with a staple, then a bobby pin. I prayed, but my prayers were never answered.

All day long, the bedrooms were locked to keep us from sleeping. Though, with the chemicals, it was almost inhuman to prevent us from it. There weren't enough chairs in the day room for all, so if you weren't quick you would spend the day on the floor, either sitting on it or pacing on it.

I kept looking out the barred windows. I wanted to walk through wilderness and desert. Just to walk free, to climb rocks, to traverse sandy beaches while being chased by waves. I could see a street, cars busily facilitating lives; they probably didn't even think of the life they were passing by as they were swept along, confident in reality.

Objects began to threaten me in that they existed too strongly. An ashtray. A chair. A clock. They refused to be ignored and thrust themselves upon my consciousness. A table, for instance, so full of meaning and being that it consumed my every thought and perception. I became alone in the world with each object, one by one. Their imposition was almost unbearable.

Every time I would leave the ward to go outside, even to the fenced-in patio, I would be overcome with the feeling that I was going to explode. The world was too great, too huge; I would fly apart without any boundaries to contain me.

I couldn't tell if I had to go to the bathroom, if I was going to be incontinent or very confusedly wondered if it was someone else who had the need to relieve themselves that I was now feeling.

I knew the only way out was the complete destruction of myself. If this could not be done physically, then I had to somehow ravage everything that made me "me"—made me capable of feeling and of feeling alone.

33

THE SUNDAY TIMES

"Hi, I'm Billy. What's your name?"

That is how he approached everyone, with gentle invitation.

He had a son on another coast. He spoke of his son playing soccer, watching birds instead of the ball and examining cloud formations instead of strategizing about the game. Billy would watch and say, "That's my son." He talked with so much pride about his boy. He appreciated the dreamer in a person.

Billy liked to get the *New York Times* on a Sunday morning and read while drinking coffee with cream and Bloody Marys with their stalks of celery. He enjoyed reading very much and other such cultural endeavors, plays, ballets, films. But when asked to comment he always said, "I'm a barbarian."

Many times we would go to an all-night diner—Queues. I would get coffee and he would get a huge platter o' fries with white gravy. We would talk until the sun rose, admire the rising, then go home to sleep.

It was around this time that Billy began actively to kill himself. And I didn't know how to stop him. He took a taxi up to a skiing resort and spent the night there lying in the snow with nothing for warmth. He didn't die; he shook violently all night, yet endured. He hitchhiked home. He was not defeated by this failure.

I was sad that I had languished so many years in mental hospitals. He told me that that time was not wasted. He said there was something there to learn, but he stressed that any more would be overkill. He promised then that he would rescue me if they tried to take me back again to the hospital. I trusted him.

He managed to open up a small new and used bookstore on the bus mall. He was born to such a job, and he loved it. But mental illness crept back to him; he hated life (especially life as a mental patient). He stood on a roadside trying to gain strength to jump in front of a truck. He stood there for several hours, but this course was unworkable.

We drank strawberry margaritas at a sidewalk café, conversing easily. From there we went to a park to watch a concert; we stood outside the fence and enjoyed very much. We passed afternoons watching independent films and drinking white wine in a theater/pub.

We spent so much time together and spontaneously weakened in the wake of each other. Now we both wanted to die. The doctor wanted Billy to go to a hospital. Billy replied that a hospital is no venue in which to achieve mental health, especially to eliminate profound sorrow. He said there should be places with cut flowers and classical music with works of art on the walls and conversations on philosophy. The doctor let Billy go free. My doctor thought only to ensure my safety and indeed committed me to the state hospital. I waited for Billy. He had promised to rescue me: all I had to do was get a pass and Billy and I would go free, either to live a Life or to die.

A social worker took me into a small room. Billy was dead. He had jumped off the appropriately nick-named Suicide Bridge. I laughed. He had done it. But why hadn't that bastard taken me? Now he was happy and I alone.

I miss him.

34

SUICIDE

It was surprisingly easy to open my wrists, and taking all those pills wasn't tremendously difficult either.

I had earlier in the day attempted to buy a gun. I picked out a friendly gun, not too cumbersome but definitely one to get the job done. I filled out the form. The clerk glanced at the form and seemed to yell, "You're mentally defective?"

I stared. I hadn't lied on the form; I didn't think my hospitalizations would matter a lot.

"You've been court committed?" he challenged.

I nodded.

"You can't buy a gun. That's the law!"

Heads throughout the store turned to look at the maniac at the gun counter. I walked out stunned.

I didn't know what to do next. I had been so completely sure that I would be dead in a matter of hours. I bought flowers—irises and daffodils. I took them home and put them in a tall white vase with an aspirin in the water to prevent wilting.

I performed tasks that needed attending—dishes, dusting, I showered. I was dead, my body just hadn't realized it yet.

I thought of the pills, the ones that the drug book warned should be monitored with suicidal people; I thought of the razor. I had dipped it in my arms, my legs, my breasts; now I just needed to do the same on my wrists. It would be both simultaneously, I decided. Orange juice for the pills and supine in the bathtub to catch all drops of blood. I wanted, coveted this leaving; I was desperate.

Music to die by — Brahms' *Fourth*. Soothe myself senseless. Never recover. I became increasingly sleepy. One finishing, eternal sleep. I didn't want to see God. I hoped not to be punished. All I wanted was a deep, dreamless and everlasting sleep.

More blood escaped me than I thought possible. Then I started to sleep. I closed my eyes on voices, on worries, on life — for the last time.

I awoke. On orienting myself in the hospital, my first feelings were of disbelief, horror, devastation.

"This isn't possible! How? Who did this to me?" I had been so certain this would never happen. A kind of shock set in.

Now, not only was I alive with the misery intrinsic in that, but further agonized that now I would be in the hospital. Failure. Failure complete.

I was deprived of everything. Only a hospital gown I had. No cutlery (not even plastic), I was served only finger food. No pencils or pens. (I might stab my eyes out.) No access to a phone. (I had repeatedly called 9-1-1 for help.) My bathroom door was unlocked only long enough for me to relieve myself. No glass of any kind—perfume bottles, mirrors, jars of hand cream. No bobby pins, no jewelry, no makeup, no toiletries, not even a comb. Nothing. My hospital gown and a mark on the floor that ESP-ed kind and comforting words into my head. I called this mark my Frangilator; I would lie on the floor and commune with it for hours.

The floor—I needed to constantly be on the floor (preferably the floor in the bathroom). I wasn't safe standing or sitting on a chair. I needed to rock myself. I needed darkness. I needed to die.

35

THE STATE HOSPITAL, AGAIN

A large room with strange people, many at the table. A man said they were trying to determine if I was in need of hospitalization again. I just wanted to go home. I recognized one of those stone persons as my doctor—a doctor who had given up on me years ago. I was frightened and very cold. I began to realize that I was slipping into Can't Move Sickness. I stayed bundled in my hospital-lent blanket, shivering in the August heat. My only reply to the questions speeding by me was "I'm scared." They committed me.

When I got back to the hospital, the patients were gathered to sing "Amazing Grace." It was tremendously hot. Lights and shadows danced about me. And I was unable to determine the vitality of black spots and other assorted marks on the floors and furniture; they became Frangilators.

I smoked and smoked, looking for an in with reality. I had to sit through another tedious, redundant search of my belongings, yet I was nervous and bit my nails to the quick as they took item after item away from me, listing all the reasons that I couldn't have them—you could cut yourself with that, you could stab your eyes with that, that would be poisonous if ingested… I knew well enough that the items they removed would be lost by the time I could have them back. My clothes were sent to be permanently marked with my name and the name of the hospital.

Finally, secured in the hideous and dirty ward, I circled the room at a furious pace. Voices of demons and angels fell into my head from the diaphanous, overhead protection from blue. They condemned me, taunted me, and when at last I ventured a soul-screaming reply, they destroyed me.

I regained a timeline in a small bed, an empty room. My limbs tied to a bed frame.

"I'm not your puppet on a string," I replied to an errant voice.

I watched, mesmerized by the spatial equations that resolved themselves in the light fixture that stared at my eyes.

An ache in my bladder made me wonder who had to go to the bathroom. Uncomfortable urgency, please go to the bathroom! Yes, it must be the nurse that has to urinate. Why doesn't she go? I don't think I can hold it very much longer. I can't do it; I can't leave this small, dark chamber.

Eventually, I found myself seated on a torn lime-green vinyl chair by the television. So severely controlled was I that it hurt.

"I'm totally controlled, and they're beaming x-rays at me from the clinic upstairs," I explained to someone in the nurse's station.

"Do you want a PRN?" asked this someone.

"No!" I cried, alarmed. "I want them to stop killing me!"

"I'll talk to you when you can make sense."

Hours hung in the heavy air like the ball of the summer sun. Flies buzzed everywhere; they were caught in the sticky strips of paper hanging from the ceiling. Patients were lying, in various stages of lucidity, around the courtyard. Some yelled. Some listened to a borrowed radio, some just sat and rocked themselves, back and forth, back and forth. And all (unless sleeping) smoked. And smoked. The currency in hospitals is cigarettes; I've seen women trade their diamond wedding rings for five cigarettes. People constantly begged for them or for anything else they saw that they wanted. And no matter how insignificant the item, if you didn't want it stolen you had to keep it locked up.

Every day was a struggle for me. I tried hard to remember the past; I needed to convince myself that I had truly once lived. Life seemed so remote and unreal. Had I really done those things? Had I been that brave?

I understood suicide as few who remain alive do. I've lain in a bed barely moving for weeks, even when being there so long caused physical pain. So incapacitated was I that trips to the bathroom required dedication. Days went by without my noticing that the sun had shone, nor could I appreciate the velvety texture of night's cloak. Weeks where reality was a gray void.

To notice the sun would have been a knife ripping into the swollen sack of poison that was my heart, and the poison, seeping out, would have killed me.

Life was confusion and life was certainty. Confused by "What am I doing here?" and certain that the doors would stay locked.

But once, the always-locked door swung open and a woman came in. I happened to pass by before it swung closed. I understood this open door to be a sign from God that I should leave. So, I left the ward. No one saw me leave; I walked down a long corridor and eventually I came to a door to the out-side — a parking lot. The bright day was insufferably hot. I walked out to the street. There were only fields on all sides; I didn't know where I could, should or even wanted to go. I spotted a young couple, they ESP-ed me to follow them (another sign from God). Presently, I was back in real civilization. A strip mall with a large grocery store.

I went in hoping to find cigarettes. I couldn't identify many items because the colors were too intense and they existed too strongly. But my nicotine-addicted body spotted a shelf of tobacco products. I had only the clothes I was wearing, so of course no money, it had not occurred to me that I needed any, and here were all the cigarettes I could need! I opened a carton and removed a pack. I asked the cashier for matches; she gave me two books. I quitted the store.

The sweltering heat drove me to seek shade. I sat next to a big building that was painted red. I sat there enjoying my cigarettes, for a time. I was soon to be aware of a rampant thirst. Thirst so bad I thought I might be dying. I found a telephone and called my mother. She came quite quickly. And I enjoyed a tall glass of cold water. But then it was the hospital again.

"Snake!" the massive woman screamed. "Tonight, you die! You can't get away with what you did to me."

The object of her wrath sat placidly by, staring at tiny, newly hatched birds in their nearby nest while singing loudly "America the Beautiful" and seemingly enjoying the afternoon sun while urine poured down her bare legs.

The sun shone down, casting everything in a brilliant golden-green light. The heavy day dragged on interminably (as they all did). The sounds of the harvest of nearby corn lulled most of the patients to peace. I watched the woman who was screaming; her name was Bea. She was huge and lacked any semblance of modesty. Watching the spectacle made me nervous. I was always careful to avoid being noticed and I dreaded even a mild argument. Bea always screamed incoherently at staff or patients — whoever was handy. She called me Kris Thigpen and swore that I wouldn't get away with burning down her restaurant in San Francisco. Bea was the only person in this hospital who made me feel afraid.

Sometimes the world/ward seemed so safe, during the day when all the spiders and demons stayed in the shadows. All I could see were lights and shadows, sometimes only swirls of color.

These conditions were acceptable to me. I tried to make my own movements and to make smooth transitions of thought, without the computer. I found it difficult to translate my thoughts (which manifested themselves in feeling) into words. My inability to articulate often resulted in confusion on my doctors' part and nearly always seemed to defeat my purposes.

I could sit comfortably by the hour rocking, smoking, absorbing heat... listening to voices. Always voices, yet always loneliness.

Again and again, the promises made by doctors that I would be released in a few months came to nothing. My great achievement in independence was being transferred to a group home on the hospital grounds. It was lovely to be able to walk the grounds during the day and in the beginning hours of darkness. And I could earn some money sorting the hospital's recycling and crushing cans; the money was good for biweekly trips to neighborhood shopping centers, and we could order delivery pizza.

But it was the same (for all purposes) as the hospital. The views were the same; the food was the same; the medications were the same—the same pills smashed into the same pudding to be spooned down our unwilling throats.

I could physically no longer contemplate Life. It was gone.

36

LOST IN ILLNESS

Person upon person, my friends found different lives. Some slipped away; others left intentionally, abandoning me. They all left without good-byes, crazy people probably don't notice, they likely reasoned. I have most often wondered about Kay. I haven't seen her since my Life ended. I've heard that she's become a psychiatric nurse. I want to send her yellow flowers. She understands Death.

Are my inmates friends? We've fought and comforted, I've lived for years with all their raving and counter-raving, and they with mine. These women are my family; they make me feel safer.

I lived several lifetimes in my first twenty-one years, perhaps that's why I was deprived of more. Years have passed me comatose, neither the years nor I waited. I want now another chance, but I'm old now. The time to take chances has passed.

I realize that my biggest crime (I've committed many small infractions)—what I shall surely be held accountable for in the end—is a wasted Life. I can't remember how this happened to me. So many years ago, voices held me back, and since I couldn't quit them, I quit Life.

Acknowledgements

Having *Possums Run Amok* published is the most glorious achievement in my life. And my story would not have been written if not for Ben Moorad. Thank you, Ben. To say that you believed in me and encouraged me doesn't say enough. I felt like I needed permission to write. You gave me the confidence to recognize that I, my story and my writing have worth. You drew me into a life of writing. I am forever grateful to you for that.

Carla Girard, many thanks to you as well. You saw the potential in my book, championed it and worked to publish it, and did so beautifully. And I'm so very happy that you're my friend.

Thanks to my brothers and sister—Dave and John and Andrea, for keeping your annoyance at bay and putting up with my oddities, for being happy for me and my writing and giving me a soft place to fall.

Thanks to Ki Von Schiller (or Slithy T, as I call her), for bringing happiness and adventure and true camaraderie into my life.

About the Author

Lora Lafayette's award-winning poems and stories have appeared in *PLAZM Magazine*, *The Buckman Journal*, *Pen & Ink*, and others.

Lora continues to struggle with mental health issues but is receiving very good care and support from her healthcare providers, family and friends. She still travels the world, though not quite so frenetically as she used to. Lora is a Northwest native and currently lives in downtown Portland, Oregon, with Finn, who purrs.